the prayer

JOURNAL

DAILY STEPS TOWARD
PRAYING GOD'S HEART

Compiled by Dean Ridings

This prayer journal belongs to

_____

and is for the year

_____

A NavPress resource published in alliance
with Tyndale House Publishers, Inc.

NavPress is the publishing ministry of The Navigators, an international Christian organization and leader in personal spiritual development. NavPress is committed to helping people grow spiritually and enjoy lives of meaning and hope through personal and group resources that are biblically rooted, culturally relevant, and highly practical.

For more information, visit www.NavPress.com.

For information about special discounts for bulk purchases, please contact Tyndale House Publishers at csresponse@tyndale.com, or call 1-800-323-9400.

ISBN 978-1-57683-616-3

Printed in China

24 23 22 21 20 19 18
19 18 17 16 15 14 13

Table of contents

introduction

Taking God at His word transformed the life and ministry of a young man named Dawson Trotman. Dawson was deep into Scripture memory. One verse that captured his attention was Jeremiah 33:3, "Call unto me, and I will answer thee, and shew thee great and mighty things, which thou knowest not" (KJV).

Again and again he reviewed and meditated upon this verse. *Did God really mean it—call upon Me; I will answer you; I will show you great and mighty things?* Pondering this led to a 42-day "prayer meeting," in which Dawson and a few others with him got serious about praying for local youth and cities, and then expanded out to other cities in their state, other states in their nation, and finally the world.

The small band of brothers prayed for two hours every morning—three on Sundays! In six weeks' time, they had spent more than 100 hours in prayer, asking God to use them to win and train individuals for His glory around the world. They didn't know how, but they claimed Jeremiah 33:3 and trusted God to fill in the details.

"We didn't even know what we were praying," Dawson said. "I didn't realize that within four years, men from every state of the nation would walk into our front room and find the Savior. God answered our prayers abundantly, and there was the beginning of our work called today by the name, Navigators."

This prayer journal is especially designed to help you conduct an extended "prayer meeting" of your own. It is designed both to help you connect with God more deeply, and to learn to pray what is on God's own heart.

You will grow in intimacy with God as you take time out to talk with Him each day. In this journal you will find places to "carry on the conversation" as you write weekly and daily prayer requests. This will help you become more intentional as you approach the most important conversation of the day—with the Creator of the universe who is there, cares, and listens with an ear to respond both for His glory and your good.

You will grow in intimacy with God as you give prayerful consideration to the daily Bible readings. This journal includes "The Book-at-a-Time Bible Reading Plan," a fresh way to walk through God's Word in a year, developed by Mark Bogart and Peter Mayberry. From time to time you will find a call to reflect upon what you have read and how the Lord has led.

You will grow in intimacy with God as you tap into the helps included: weekly Scripture verses and select readings—mostly favorites adapted from *Pray!* magazine—to help guide you toward that deep, abiding relationship with God that Jesus spoke of in John 15, plus helpful resources in the back to guide you as you "continue the journey."

Through the years, using a prayer journal has been a personal blessing. I have grown in my passion for Christ through prayer, which is what *Pray!* magazine is all about. My prayer is that this will also be your experience as you allow the Holy Spirit to guide you on this journey.

weekLy Requests

"If my people, who are called by my name,

will humble themselves and pray

and seek my face and turn from their wicked ways,

then will I hear from heaven and will forgive their sin

and will heal their land."

(2 Chronicles 7:14)

The following pages provide space to write down the names of people and situations and circumstances for which you want to pray regularly. We have provided a format that focuses on a different category each day, but don't be bound by that if you desire to pray for a group on a daily basis. As you use this journal, go back to those lists as often as you are led. If God gives you a Scripture to pray for someone, jot it next to his or her name.

Monday

Pray for Your Family

List the name of each member of your family. If you are married, include your spouse's family members. When there's a new addition to the family—a birth, marriage, adoption—add the name to the list. Every week entrust each one to the Lord, perhaps praying a promise from Scripture on his or her behalf (e.g., "Thank you that _____ is Your workmanship, created in You to do good works, which You have prepared in advance for _____ to do," Ephesians 2:10). Pray that God will bless, guide, keep, and use them, meet them at their point of need, and draw them ever one step closer to Jesus Christ. Thank the Lord for what He has done, is doing, and will do in their lives.

Name   Verse to Pray

_____   _____

_____   _____

_____   _____

_____   _____

_____   _____

_____   _____

_____   _____

_____   _____

_____   _____

_____   _____

_____   _____

_____   _____

_____   _____

_____   _____

_____   _____

_____   _____

_____   _____

Tuesday

Pray for God's Family

Pray for the body of Christ. Start with the local body, your church. List the names of your church's pastor(s), ministry leaders (e.g., elders, deacons, Sunday school teachers, nursery workers), and their spouses and children for whom you feel compelled to pray. List other members of your church for whom you have committed to pray. Add to the list the missionaries you support. Pray that the gospel is proclaimed "as of first importance" (see 1 Corinthians 15:1-11). Pray that the Lord will bless, guide, keep, and use each one, and for any specific needs. Pray for nationally known Christian leaders, parachurch ministries and their leadership, all lay-workers seeking to be "salt and light" in their communities. "Keep on praying for all the saints" (Ephesians 6:18)!

Name   Verse to Pray

_____   _____

_____   _____

_____   _____

_____   _____

_____   _____

_____   _____

_____   _____

_____   _____

_____   _____

_____   _____

_____   _____

_____   _____

_____   _____

_____   _____

_____   _____

_____   _____

wednesday

pray for your community

"Who is my neighbor?" someone once asked Jesus. The Lord responded with the Parable of the Good Samaritan (see Luke 10:25-37). The essence of this parable is, "What happens to you matters to me." This should guide our prayers for people in our communities—those we live near, work with, bump into at school, see at the mall, and so forth. List the names of people in the various communities in which you are an "insider." Pray that the Lord will meet each one at his or her point of need, both physical and spiritual, according to His will. May each one know the truth of John 10:10, "The thief comes only to steal and kill and destroy; I have come that they may have life, and have it to the full."

Name	Verse to Pray

Thursday

Pray for Your Nation

A most fitting prayer to pray on behalf of the nation is to adapt the Lord's words in 2 Chronicles 7:14, that His people, who are called by His name, will humble themselves and pray and seek His face and turn from their wicked ways—then He will hear from heaven, forgive their sin, and heal their land. Pray for the revival of God's people in the nation, that they will be "Jesus in jeans" to the people in their communities, being used of God to lead others ever one step closer to Him. Ask God's forgiveness for the nation's sins of pride, prejudice, insensitivity to the needs and hurts of others. List local and national spiritual and political leaders and pray for each. List and pray about current national issues.

Name   Verse to Pray

_____   _____

_____   _____

_____   _____

_____   _____

_____   _____

_____   _____

_____   _____

_____   _____

_____   _____

_____   _____

_____   _____

_____   _____

_____   _____

_____   _____

_____   _____

_____   _____

_____   _____

Friday

Pray for the world

Pray for a worldwide outpouring of the Holy Spirit, and thus a vibrant body of Christ being used of God to help people "to know Christ and to make Him known." Pray that revived believers would reach out and touch people for Christ, meeting their physical and spiritual needs, as Jesus' early church followers did (see Acts 3:1-10), and that they would respond with His love, grace, compassion, and wisdom to social struggles (add to your prayer list needs you are aware of). Pray for the nations of the 10/40 Window, which extends from West Africa to East Asia and is home to the world's neediest people, least evangelized nations, and major world religions. Pray for the persecuted church. Finally, pray for the advance of the gospel everywhere (see Matthew 24:14).

Name   Verse to Pray

_____   _____

_____   _____

_____   _____

_____   _____

_____   _____

_____   _____

_____   _____

_____   _____

_____   _____

_____   _____

_____   _____

_____   _____

_____   _____

_____   _____

_____   _____

_____   _____

saturday

pray for the Helpless, Hopeless, Hurting, and Lost

Start with the world, draw closer to your nation, closer to your state, and closer still to your own community—and list the names of and pray for the physically and spiritually afflicted. Pray that the Lord would use believers, including you and your family, to help meet the needs of "the least of these," all who are hungry, thirsty, strangers, in need of clothes, sick, and in prison (see Matthew 25:31-46). Find out what needs exist in your community and how your church and local parachurch ministries are helping to meet those needs. List and pray for their efforts. While "every need isn't a call," some needs are. Ask God how He would want you to help.

Name   Verse to Pray

_____   _____

_____   _____

_____   _____

_____   _____

_____   _____

_____   _____

_____   _____

_____   _____

_____   _____

_____   _____

_____   _____

_____   _____

_____   _____

_____   _____

_____   _____

_____   _____

_____   _____

_____   _____

sunday

pray for personal guidance

"Do you not know that in a race all the runners run, but only one gets the prize? Run in such a way as to get the prize," said the apostle Paul (1 Corinthians 9:24). Pray that God would help you to run for the prize in every area of your personal life. List specific prayer requests for His guidance in these five key areas: personal, family, work/school, church, and community. Personalize Romans 12:1-2. Thank God for all that He has done, is doing, and will do (because He has promised!) on your behalf, such as helping you to become more and more like Jesus every day (see Philippians 1:6, Romans 8:28-29). Pray that on a daily, moment-by-moment basis you would know His presence and live in such a way as to please Him.

Request   Verse to Pray

_____   _____
_____   _____
_____   _____
_____   _____
_____   _____
_____   _____
_____   _____
_____   _____
_____   _____
_____   _____
_____   _____
_____   _____
_____   _____
_____   _____
_____   _____
_____   _____

Daily Requests

"Give ear to my words, O LORD, consider my sighing.

Listen to my cry for help, my King and my God, for to you I pray.

In the morning, O LORD, you hear my voice;

in the morning I lay my requests before you

and wait in expectation."

(Psalm 5:1-3)

January

seeking the Lord

"The secret of seeking is not in our human ascent to God, but in God's descent to us. We start out searching, but we end up being discovered. We think we are looking for something; we realize we are found by Someone. As in Francis Thompson's famous picture, 'the hound of heaven' has tracked us down. What brings us home is not our discovery of the way home but the call of the Father who has been waiting there for us all along, whose presence there makes home *home*."

—Os Guinness

Os Guinness, *The Call* (Nashville: Word Publishing, 1998), p. 14.

> They all joined together constantly in prayer, along with the women and Mary the mother of Jesus, and with his brothers.
>
> —Acts 1:14

January 1 · Genesis 1-2, Psalm 1

January 2 · Genesis 3-5, Psalm 2

personaL awakening

True awakening begins in the heart of the individual. D. L. Moody suggested that every revival in history could be traced back to a single kneeling form. British Methodist scholar and historian Dr. A. Skevington Wood says that true revival always includes "an absorbing concentration on prayer."

January 3 · Genesis 6-9, Psalm 3

January 4 · Genesis 10-11, Psalm 4

January 5 · Genesis 12-14, Psalm 5

January 6 · Genesis 15-17, Psalm 6

From the outset of the birth of the early church, prayer has been foundational to every awakening in history. The early church was born out of 10 days in prayer and was sustained through its formative years by prayer (see Acts 1:14; 4:31; 12:1-5).

A. T. Pierson wrote: "Prayer has been starting point and goal to every movement in which are the elements of personal progress. Wherever the church has been aroused and the world's wickedness arrested, somebody, somewhere, has been praying." Pray for a new consistency and fervency in seeking God in personal prayer.

—Dick Eastman
(*Pray!*, Issue 1, p. 26.)

> **Let us then approach** the throne of grace with confidence, so that we may receive mercy and find grace to help us in our time of need.
>
> —Hebrews 4:16

january 7 · *Reflection*

january 8 · Genesis 18-20, Psalm 7

come and P.R.A.Y.

Here's an acronym that will help guide you in prayer: P.R.A.Y. The letters stand for Praise, Repent, Access, and Yield, which captures the essence of prayer—to seek an audience with the King of the universe, the Holy One, who in the mystery of His character loves us and responds to our prayers.

Praise: We're to enter His gates with thanksgiving and His courts with praise (see Psalm 100:4). Sit quietly and thank

january 9 · Genesis 21-23, Psalm 8

January 10 · Genesis 24-26, Psalm 9

January 11 · Genesis 27-29, Psalm 10

January 12 · Genesis 30-32, Psalm 11

God for who He is and what He has done.

Repent: A sober reminder comes from Psalm 66:18: "If I had cherished sin in my heart, the Lord would not have listened." A spiritual cleansing is needed in order to come nearer to the throne of God.

Access: We're not telling God anything new—"All my longings lie open before you, O Lord; my sighing is not hidden from you" (Psalm 38:9). Even so, He gives us access to talk to Him about our needs and frustrations.

Yield: The fact that we have brought our prayer list before God indicates our trust that He will, in His time and in His way, show us the way we should go (see Psalm 143:8).

—Jeanne Zornes
(*Pray!*, Issue 11, p. 11.)

> "And when you **pray,** do not be like the hypocrites, for they love to pray standing in the synagogues and on the street corners to be seen by men. I tell you the truth, they have received their reward in full. But when you pray, go into your room, close the door and pray to your Father, who is unseen. Then your Father, who sees what is done in secret, will reward you."
>
> —Matthew 6:5,6

the quiet place

The first time I heard about someone's "prayer closet," I was

January 13 · Genesis 33–36, Psalm 12

January 14 · *Reflection*

January 15 · Genesis 37–39, Psalm 13

January 16 · Genesis 40-42, Psalm 14

January 17 · Genesis 43-46, Psalm 15

January 18 · Genesis 47-50, Psalm 16

amused. The thought of climbing into a closet among shoes and winter coats to pray seemed, well, ridiculous. But constant references by people of prayer to their "closets" kept me wondering if I might be missing something. So I decided to give it a try.

I selected the storage closet off my living room, a 3' x 6' space packed with boxes of old photos, blankets, and craft supplies. Soon all the boxes and cartons found new homes, and that's when I began to feel God's pleasure at having made Him a sole priority in this area of my home.

I still can—and do—pray anywhere. But real intimacy with God occurred when I came aside with Him to this quiet place.

—Sandra Higley

(*Pray!*, Issue 7, pp. 26-27.)

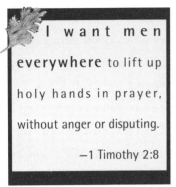

> I want men everywhere to lift up holy hands in prayer, without anger or disputing.
>
> —1 Timothy 2:8

ALL of me

Did you know that your body can seek God along with your spirit and voice? God gave you your body, and He loves it when you use it to communicate with Him! You can use many different positions, or "postures," when you pray. Each one is a way of showing God what is in your heart and asking Him to meet you there.

Kneeling shows God that you are entering into His presence or asking Him for something.

January 19 • Mark 1–3, Psalm 17

January 20 • Mark 4–6, Psalm 18:1–24

January 21 • *Reflection*

January 22 · Mark 7-9, Psalm 18:25-50

January 23 · Mark 10-12, Psalm 19

January 24 · Mark 13-16, Psalm 20

Standing shows God that you are ready for "marching orders."

Walking shows God that you are "on the move" for Him, ready for His battle plans.

Bowing shows God that you honor Him and feel humble because of who He is.

Prostrate, lying flat on your face or back, shows God that you are in awe of Him and are desperate and hungry for Him to come and be with you.

Uplifted hands show God that you are reaching toward Him—in praise or asking for something with arms open to receive it.

—Lani C. Hinkle
(*Pray*Kids!, p. 7, *Pray!* Issue 36, p. 27.)

> "And foreigners who bind themselves to the Lord to serve him, to love the name of the Lord, and to worship him, all who keep the Sabbath without desecrating it and who hold fast to my covenant—these I will bring to my holy mountain and give them joy in my house of prayer. Their burnt offerings and sacrifices will be accepted on my altar; for my house will be called a house of prayer for all nations."
>
> —Isaiah 56:6,7

House of Prayer

It's said that you can tell the popularity of the church by the number who show up on Sunday morning; you can tell the

january 25 · Exodus 1-4, Psalm 21

january 26 · Exodus 5-8, Psalm 22:1-11

january 27 · Exodus 9-11, Psalm 22:12-31

January 28 · Exodus 12-14, Psalm 23

January 29 · *Reflection*

January 30 · *Reflection*

popularity of the church's pastor by the number who show up on Sunday night; and you can tell the popularity of Jesus by the number who show up to the prayer meeting.

What has happened to our churches? You call a prayer meeting today and very few people show up. I know of a church of 5,000 in Denver called a prayer meeting and only five people came.

That's a far cry from the day a century earlier when the entire city of Denver paused for prayer—"even at the high tide of business." The January 20, 1905, *Denver Post* reported: "Seldom has such a remarkable sight been witnessed—an entire great city, in the middle of a busy weekday, bowing before the throne of heaven and asking and receiving the blessing of the King of the Universe." Oh, that believers would seek the Lord similarly today!

—Jim Weidmann
National Day of Prayer Task Force
www.nationaldayofprayer.org

january 31 · *Reflection*

monthLy RefLection

What is the Spirit of God saying to me this month? What is my response?

prayer for the month:

Lord God, I seek You with all my heart and soul. I glory in Your holy name. My heart rejoices in You. I'm seeking just one thing—let me dwell in Your presence all my life, let me gaze on Your beauty! My heart hears You say, "Come talk with Me" . . . oh, Lord, here I come! Thank You for Your love—it is evident to those who love You. I cling to Your promise that I will find You if I seek You (Deuteronomy 4:29; 1 Chronicles 16:10; Psalm 27:4,8; Proverbs 8:17).

prayers that birth revival

By Life Action Ministries

Desperate conditions frequently inspire intense times of seeking the Lord. Difficulty and uncertainty can become fertile ground for a deep and lasting movement of God's Spirit.

The following prayer guide has been written with the realization that all revivals are birthed through intercessory prayer. The prayer points focus on the corporate needs of God's people. We encourage you, as you pray, to make them personal. As a result, may you experience a fresh walk of revival in your own life and family.

"If my people, who are called by my name, will humble themselves and pray and seek my face and turn from their wicked ways, then will I hear from heaven and will forgive their sin and will heal their land" (2 Chronicles 7:14).

"If my people . . . will humble themselves"

1. Pray that we as Christians will bow our knees before the Lord at the beginning of each day, so that we may receive His grace daily to live as we should (James 4:6-10).

2. Pray that all those who have a personal relationship with the Lord will walk in a spirit of humility, as Jesus walked, and live each day in recognition that pride leads to destruction and humility precedes honor (Micah 6:8; Proverbs 18:12).

3. Pray that believers will comprehend the value of humility: that God hears the cry of the humble and delivers them, that it is better to be among the lowly than to share the wealth of the proud, and that God's presence accompanies those who are of a contrite and humble spirit (Proverbs 16:19; Isaiah 57:15).

4. Pray that each person in every Christian home (particularly husbands and wives) will be humble in spirit, in order that their prayers may be answered (1 Peter 3:7-12).

5. Pray that young Christians will be clothed with humility, respecting their elders, lifting all their concerns to God, and trusting God to exalt them at the proper time (1 Peter 5:5-10).

6. Pray that all Christians will remember, with gratitude, what they have been saved from. Pray that times of crisis would be tangible reminders of "what we deserve" apart from the mercy of God (1 Peter 3:13-17; Titus 3:1-9; Psalms 40:1-3, 68:19-20, 103:1-5).

7. Pray that God's people would assume responsibility for the moral and spiritual erosion which has permeated not only our nation but also our world (Ezra 9:6; Psalm 51:16-17).

"and pray"

8. Pray that God's people would unite in praying for all who are in authority, that we may lead quiet and peaceful lives in godliness and holiness (1 Timothy 2:1-4).

9. Pray that Christians will seek God first each day privately, before getting physically involved in His work for the day (Matthew 6:6-8,33; Psalm 32:6).

10. Pray that urgency and fervency would characterize the prayers of God's people (Isaiah 64:9).

11. Pray that our first response as Christians will be to pray when we become anxious about a situation, circumstance, or relationship (Matthew 6:25-32; Philippians 4:6-7; Jeremiah 33:3).

12. Pray that God would raise up an army of prayer warriors who are willing to persevere in prayer and wage a long war on their knees (Luke 18:1-8).

13. Pray that God would give pastors wisdom as they call their congregations to intercession and lead them to an understanding of the times (Ephesians 4:11-13; Isaiah 56:1-7; Jeremiah 23:1-4).

14. Pray for a spirit of prayer to spread like a wildfire across our land and world until every church becomes a

house of prayer, saturated with seasons and extended times of turning to the Lord (Philippians 4:6-7; Luke 18:1; Matthew 21:13).

"And seek My Face"

15. Pray that adult Christians will set a pattern of seeking the Lord in all things, so that younger generations may find their strength and hope in the Lord, especially in times of crisis (Psalms 27, 91; Acts 17:26-27).

16. Pray that God would increase our belief in His ability to intervene supernaturally and do the impossible, especially in times of crisis. Pray that we would forgo the fleshly appetites of food, entertainment, and pleasure to seek the face of God (Hebrews 11:6; Mark 9:23; James 5:16-18; Isaiah 58:6-12).

17. Pray that God's people and our national leaders would not trust in military strength, financial might and strategies, or political power and influence to solve our difficulties. Pray that the Scriptures would guide all decision-making (Zechariah 4:6; Isaiah 55:8-9, 48:17; Jeremiah 9:23-24; Psalm 147:10-11; Proverbs 21:30-31).

18. Pray that God's people would not be self-sufficient, thinking "we can handle this." May we see our dire need for help from God and others (John 15:5; 2 Corinthians 3:5; Nehemiah 6:16; Jeremiah 2:31-32).

19. Pray that God's people would lay aside their petty differences, personal agendas, and divisive attitudes and genuinely unite behind the desperate need for an outpouring of God's Spirit in revival (Psalm 133:1-3; Ephesians 4:1-6).

20. Pray that Christians will seek the face of God versus the hand of God; that our chief concern would be His approval versus His blessing; that we would place our attention and our desires on pleasing Him (Psalm 27:8; Revelation 4:11; Colossians 3:2).

21. Pray that a healthy fear of God would permeate the hearts and minds of God's people. Ask God to deliver us from the fear of man which can ensnare us (Proverbs 1:7, 9:10, 29:25).

"And Turn from Their Wicked Ways"

22. Pray that Christians will meditate daily on the Word of God, so that they may be kept pure and from sin, allowing the God of heaven to conform them to the image of Christ (Psalm 119:9-11; 1 Peter 1:13-2:3; Romans 8:29; Philippians 1:6; Hebrews 12:4-13; 2 Corinthians 7:1).

23. Pray that Christians everywhere will understand their responsibility to live blamelessly before a lost and watching world (Philippians 2:14-16).

24. Pray that God's people will honestly and immediately acknowledge their sins, seek God's forgiveness, and expose all sin appropriately (Romans 2:1-2; Galatians 6:1).

25. Pray that God's people would grieve over their own sin and how it affects a holy God (Nehemiah 9; 2 Chronicles 7:14).

26. Pray that genuine repentance would characterize the response of God's people to sin and that the lordship of Jesus Christ would rule their daily living (2 Corinthians 7:9-10; Matthew 7:21).

27. Pray for a contrite and broken spirit among believers as they become aware of sin in their lives and in their churches (Isaiah 57:15).

"Then Will I Hear from Heaven"

28. Praise God that His hand is not too short to save and that His ear is not too heavy to hear. Claim the promise that the Lord draws near to all those who call upon Him in truth (Isaiah 59:1; Psalm 145:18).

"And Will Forgive Their Sin"

29. Thank the Lord for His promise to extend mercy to those who "confess and forsake their sin." Thank Him that He is faithful and just to forgive sin and to cleanse us from all unrighteousness (Proverbs 28:13; 1 John 1:9).

"And Will Heal Their Land"

30. Praise the Lord that He promises to heal those who have fallen away, and bind up the wounds of the torn and bruised, and restore the years the locusts have eaten (Jeremiah 3:22; Hosea 6:1; Joel 2:25).

LIFE ACTION MINISTRIES challenges and encourages the church toward revival. For more information go to www.lifeaction.org. This article is taken from *Pray!*, Issue 34, p. 43. Used by permission of Life Action Ministries. To order an adaptation of this article as a full-color bookmark prayer guide (50 per pack), call 1-800-366-7788 and ask for item #250, or go to www.praymag.com.

February

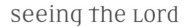

seeing the Lord

"The greatest privilege of prayer is that of coming into the actual presence of God to enjoy loving conversation and communion with Him. We are to pray frequently (1 Thessalonians 5:17) and openly (Revelation 3:20) and even 'with confidence so that we may receive mercy and find grace to help us in our time of need' (Hebrews 4:16). What an invitation! There is none other like it."

—Paul Cedar

Paul Cedar, *A Life of Prayer* (Nashville, TN: Word Publishing, 1998), p. 16.

> **For the earth** will be filled with the knowledge of the glory of the LORD, as the waters cover the sea.
>
> —Habakkuk 2:14

GLimpse His GLory

To pray for God's glory is to embark on the most exciting adventure imaginable. To better understand and pray for God's glory, here are three key elements from Scripture:

• **God's glory as ESSENCE: All that God is—His character, attributes, and ways.** John wrote that when Jesus became flesh and dwelt among us, we saw His glory, full of grace and truth (John 1:14).

february 1 · Exodus 15-17, Proverbs 1

february 2 · Exodus 18-20, Proverbs 2

february 3 · Exodus 21-24, Proverbs 3

february 4 · Exodus 25-27, Proverbs 4

february 5 · Exodus 28-31, Proverbs 5

february 6 · Exodus 32-34, Proverbs 6

• **God's glory as EXHIBITION: The ways in which He reveals Himself.** The greatest manifestation of God's glory was seen in Jesus, who was the radiance of the Father's glory. We are born again when God shines His glory in the face of Christ into our hearts (2 Corinthians 4:6; Hebrews 1:3).

• **God's glory as EXALTATION: Man's response to God's glory.** Isaiah saw God's glory in the temple and was humbly readied for the mission field. The shepherds saw God's glory and fell down to worship. We glorify God or give Him glory by the ways we respond when we experience His worth (Isaiah 6:1-8; Mark 9:5; Luke 2:9).

—Tricia McCary Rhodes
(*Pray!*, Issue 35, p. 32.)

> **You have made known to me** the path of life; you will fill me with joy in your presence, with eternal pleasures at your right hand.
>
> —Psalm 16:11

FEBRUARY 7 · *Reflection*

FEBRUARY 8 · Exodus 35-37, Proverbs 7

IN HIS PRESENCE

When I pray from a position of desperation, I am on the ledge, waiting for the Shepherd to come. I look up, longing for His face to appear. Then, suddenly, I feel His presence, beckoning me to reach my own feeble limbs toward His already outstretched hand. My finite desire meets God's infinite compassion, and He holds me, sustaining my

FEBRUARY 9 · Exodus 38-40, Proverbs 8

february 10 · Acts 1-3, Proverbs 9

february 11 · Acts 4-6, Proverbs 10:1-16

february 12 · Acts 7-9, Proverbs 10:17-32

ability to stay in His presence. That's when I feel most alive!

Prayer brings God's true nature to our awareness. Without it, I am blind to the brightness of His flame, unmoved by His out-stretched hand, and deaf to His still small voice—with only a rational understanding of Him. But when I am desperate for God's divine touch, He goes beyond the intellect and reaches the emotions.

—Kevin Young

(*Pray!*, Issue 34, p. 40.)

> **One day Jesus was praying** in a certain place. When he finished, one of his disciples said to him, "Lord, teach us to pray, just as John taught his disciples."
>
> —Luke 11:1

february 13 · Acts 10-12, Proverbs 11:1-15

february 14 · *Reflection*

february 15 · Acts 13-15, Proverbs 11:16-31

Eyes on the Master

"Lord, teach us to pray" was first whispered by a disciple as they had caught Jesus praying. The disciples looked on in utter adoration, gazing in opened-mouthed amazement at Jesus

february 16 · Acts 16-18, Proverbs 12:1-14

february 17 · Acts 19-21, Proverbs 12:15-28

february 18 · Acts 22-25, Proverbs 13:1-12

talking with His Father. They had never seen anyone pray like this before.

Perhaps it was His passion or intensity. Maybe it was His persistence, or the priority He gave to His time with the Father. It might have been the visible effect His prayer brought to His countenance. Or it may have been the results: Jesus received answers to His prayers!

We can't be sure what first attracted the disciples to beg, "Lord, teach us to pray." But seeing Jesus pray and hearing His answer would prove to be a defining moment, for both their personal lives and their ministries.

—Fred A. Hartley III
(*Pray!*, Issue 36, p. 17.)

When Mary reached the place where Jesus was and saw him, she fell at his feet and said, "Lord, if you had been here, my brother would not have died." When Jesus saw her weeping, and the Jews who had come along with her also weeping, he was deeply moved in spirit and troubled.

—John 11:32,33

Face to Face

As Jesus came to the home of Mary and Martha, it was Martha who first ran to Him and said, "Lord, if you had been here, my

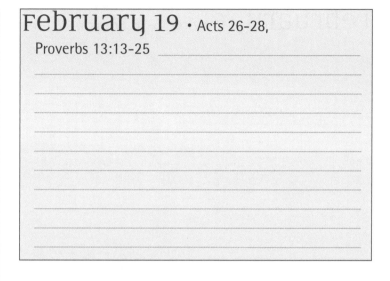

February 19 · Acts 26-28,
Proverbs 13:13-25

February 20 · Leviticus 1-4,
Proverbs 14:1-18

February 21 · *Reflection*

February 22 · Leviticus 5-8,
Proverbs 14:19-35

February 23 · Leviticus 9-11,
Proverbs 15:1-17

February 24 · Leviticus 12-14,
Proverbs 15:18-33

brother would not have died" (John 11:21). Jesus responded with the great theological truth: "I am the resurrection and the life."

Next, Mary came out to meet Jesus and made the same statement: "Lord, if you had been here, my brother would not have died." But Mary—the one who had sat at Jesus' feet before, listening to Him, meditating, and contemplating—threw herself at her Lord's feet as she said this. Jesus didn't respond to her with a sermon. Instead, He wept with her. There was an intimacy between them that enabled Him to weep instead of preach.

I want to be the intimate friend with whom Jesus weeps.

—Linda Corbin
(*Pray!*, Issue 36, p. 44.)

> **Jabez cried out** to the God of Israel, "Oh, that you would bless me and enlarge my territory! Let your hand be with me, and keep me from harm so that I will be free from pain." And God granted his request.
>
> —1 Chronicles 4:10

february 25 • Leviticus 15-18, Proverbs 16:1-16

february 26 • Leviticus 19-21, Proverbs 16:17-33

GOD IS THE BLESSING

The prayer of Jabez, hidden among a plethora of genealogies, has erupted from obscurity to popularity in recent years. As God heard Jabez and responded to his prayer, He will

february 27 • Leviticus 22-24, Proverbs 17:1-14

february 28 · Leviticus 25-27,
Proverbs 17:15-28

february (29) · *Reflection*

notes

do the same for us. One of the greatest miracles of God—granting what we pray—lies not in what He does for us, but in the way He draws near to us when we pray.

Indeed, that is the answer we all need. Ultimately, *God Himself* is the blessing. He is our portion and our territory. As the apostle Paul declared in Acts 17:28, truly it is "in him we live and move and have our being."

Lives are being changed even today through the process of praying the Jabez prayer. God's blessings are flowing . . . Why? Because the God of Jabez is our God, too—and He gives Himself in answer to our prayers. We cannot even imagine what that will look like or how wonderful it will be!

—Jacquie Tyre
(*Pray!*, Issue 25, pp. 30-32.)

notes

_____
_____
_____
_____
_____
_____
_____
_____
_____
_____

monthly reflection

What is the Spirit of God saying to me this month? What is my response?

_____
_____
_____
_____
_____
_____
_____
_____
_____
_____
_____

prayer for the month:

Open my eyes, Lord; give me sight! Show me whatever part of Your glory I can contain.

Enlighten the spiritual eyes of my heart so that I may know the hope You called me to—

the riches You've lavished on me and the great power You've given me as a believer. Bless

me with eyes that see and ears that hear (2 Kings 6:17; Exodus 33:18-23; Ephesians

1:18,19; Matthew 13:16).

March

yielding your heart

"When we know the depth of our need for God and when we are convinced that God's purpose is far superior to our preference, then we are ready to yield to God and to do God's will. 'Your will be done' is a prayer that God will bridle us and direct us, wherever that may lead."

—Brian J. Dodd

Brian J. Dodd, *Praying Jesus' Way* (Downers Grove, IL: InterVarsity Press, 1997), p. 77.

> **Therefore, I urge you,** brothers, in view of God's mercy, to offer your bodies as living sacrifices, holy and pleasing to God—this is your spiritual act of worship. Do not conform any longer to the pattern of this world, but be transformed by the renewing of your mind. Then you will be able to test and approve what God's will is—his good, pleasing and perfect will.
>
> —Romans 12:1,2

seeking god's wiLL

George Mueller cared for thousands of orphans in England during the latter half of the 19th

march 1 • Hebrews 1-3, Psalm 24

march 2 • Hebrews 4-6, Psalm 25

march 3 • Hebrews 7-10, Psalm 26

march 4 · Hebrews 11-13, Psalm 27

march 5 · Numbers 1-3, Psalm 28

march 6 · Numbers 4-7, Psalm 29

century. Known as a man of prayer, his plan for determining the will of God is a helpful outline to follow as we yield our hearts before the Lord in prayer.

1. I seek at the beginning to get my heart into such a state that it has no will of its own in regard to a given matter.

2. Having done this, I do not leave the result to feeling or simple impression. If I do so, I make myself liable to great delusions.

3. I seek the will of the Spirit through, or in connection with, the Word of God.

4. Next, I take into account providential circumstances. These often plainly indicate God's will in connection with His Word and Spirit.

5. I ask God in prayer to reveal His will to me aright.

6. Thus, through prayer to God, the study of the Word, and reflection, I come to a deliberate judgment according to the best of my ability and knowledge.

—Dick Eastman
(*Pray!*, Issue 13, p. 17.)

> **What causes fights and quarrels among you?** Don't they come from your desires that battle within you? You want something but don't get it. You kill and covet, but you cannot have what you want. You quarrel and fight. You do not have, because you do not ask God. When you ask, you do not receive, because you ask with wrong motives, that you may spend what you get on your pleasures.
>
> —James 4:1-3

motive check

We may earnestly desire God's glory. We may pour our lives into serving others for His sake. Still, we have to admit that, try as we might to avoid doing so, our own agendas taint our prayers. What can we do about these mixed motives?

march 7 · *Reflection*

march 8 · Numbers 8-10, Psalm 30

march 9 · Numbers 11-14, Psalm 31

march 10 · Numbers 15-17, Psalm 32

march 11 · Numbers 18-21, Psalm 33

march 12 · Numbers 22-24, Psalm 34

Let God search you. When we pray for God to cleanse our hearts and our motives as David did in Psalm 139:23-24, it is important to yield the search-and-destroy mission to Him. He will bring wrong motives to our attention and lead us into repentance.

Confess mixed motives. Ignoring them won't make them go away. While they may always lurk, Jesus invites us to confess them and receive forgiveness and cleansing (1 John 1:9).

Ask God to teach you. As we surrender to His refining hand, we can ask Him to redirect our hearts and cause pure motives to rise to the surface (as the psalmist did in Psalm 119:36).

Affirm that you desire His glory. Pray Scriptures such as: "your name and renown are the desire of our hearts" (Isaiah 26:8) or "O LORD, not to us but to your name be the glory" (Psalm 115:1).

Grow in thanksgiving. When we thank Him, we're not looking for anything from Him. We're focusing on Him and thanking Him out of a heart that's full from what He's given.

—Janet Leighton
(*Pray!*, Issue 16, p. 20.)

> "Brace yourself like a man; I will question you, and you shall answer me. . . ."
>
> Brace yourself like a man; I will question you, and you shall answer me. . . . "
>
> "You said, 'Listen now, and I will speak; I will question you, and you shall answer me.'"
>
> —Job 38:3, 40:7, 42:4

LET GOD ASK

Our natural tendency is to ask God why He does what He does. We think He owes us an explanation. It is the master, though, who questions the servant, not the other way around. In the book of Job, on several occasions

MARCH 13 • Numbers 25-27, Psalm 35

MARCH 14 • *Reflection*

MARCH 15 • Numbers 28-30, Psalm 36

march 16 · Numbers 31-33, Psalm 37:1-22

march 17 · Numbers 34-36, Psalm 37:23-40

march 18 · Galatians 1-3, Psalm 38

it was God who turned the tables on Job and did the questioning.

During your quiet time this week, open your heart to God and allow Him to ask you the questions. What would He ask about your time, your secret attitudes, your goals, your pain, or your fears? What are you giving your life to?

When we allow God to interrogate us, instead of the other way around, we put Him back in His rightful place as Lord.

—Randy D. Raysbrook
(*23 Ways to Jump-Start Your Spiritual Battery* by Randy D. Raysbrook, © 1996, Dawson Media. Used with permission.)

> "When you fast, do not look somber as the hypocrites do, for they disfigure their faces to show men they are fasting. I tell you the truth, they have received their reward in full. But when you fast, put oil on your head and wash your face, so that it will not be obvious to men that you are fasting, but only to your Father, who is unseen; and your Father, who sees what is done in secret, will reward you."
>
> —Matthew 6:16-18

why fast?

In his book *The Coming Revival: America's Call to Fast, Pray, and "Seek God's Face,"* Bill Bright offers seven reasons to fast:

march 19 · Galatians 4-6, Psalm 39

march 20 · Deuteronomy 1-4, Psalm 40

march 21 · *Reflection*

march 22 · Deuteronomy 5-7, Psalm 41

_____
_____
_____
_____
_____
_____
_____
_____
_____
_____
_____

march 23 · Deuteronomy 8-10, Psalm 42

_____
_____
_____
_____
_____
_____
_____
_____
_____
_____
_____

march 24 · Deuteronomy 11-13, Psalm 43

_____
_____
_____
_____
_____
_____
_____
_____
_____
_____
_____

1. Fasting is a primary means of restoration. By humbling us, fasting releases the Holy Spirit to do His revival work within us. This takes us deeper into the Christlife and gives us a greater awareness of God's reality and presence in our lives.

2. Fasting reduces the power of self so that the Holy Spirit can do a more intense work within us.

3. Fasting helps to purify us spiritually.

4. Fasting increases our spiritual reception by quieting our minds and emotions.

5. Fasting brings a yieldedness, even a holy brokenness, resulting in an inner calm and self-control.

6. Fasting renews spiritual vision.

7. Fasting inspires determination to follow God's revealed plan for our lives.

—Bill Bright
(_Pray!_, Issue 3, p. 29.)

"**Though the fig tree** does not bud and there are no grapes on the vines, though the olive crop fails and the fields produce no food, though there are no sheep in the pen and no cattle in the stalls, yet I will rejoice in the LORD, I will be joyful in God my Savior. The Sovereign LORD is my strength; he makes my feet like the feet of a deer, he enables me to go on the heights."

—Habakkuk 3:17-19

GRAPPLING WITH GOD

It's said that Habakkuk means "wrestler," and the prophet sure did grapple with God. He saw

MARCH 25 • Deuteronomy 14-16, Psalm 44

MARCH 26 • Deuteronomy 17-19, Psalm 45

MARCH 27 • Deuteronomy 20-22, Psalm 46

march 28 · Deuteronomy 23-26, Psalm 47

march 29 · *Reflection*

march 30 · *Reflection*

fellow Hebrews worshiping idols and sacrificing their children to foreign gods, and he cried out for justice. But it seemed his prayers weren't getting through.

The short book of Habakkuk records the "wrestling match," even when the Lord did answer and it wasn't what the prophet had prayed for. But by the third chapter, observe and be encouraged in your own prayer life by the prophet's new view and renewed trust.

Habakkuk stopped looking around and started seeing things from God's perspective. He resolved to live by faith in light of who God is, what He has done and is doing, and what He has promised to do—not only in the world, but also in his own life.

Are you grappling with God? Let Jesus' prayer be yours: "not my will, but yours be done" (Luke 22:42). And let Him know you agree that the Father knows best.

—Dean Ridings

march 31 · *Reflection*

monthly reflection
What is the Spirit of God saying to me this month? What is my response?

prayer for the month:

Search me, O God. Inspect every inch of my heart—may every meditation, every thought be pleasing to You. Teach me to love You with all my heart and soul. When I consider what great things You have done for me, how else can I respond but to serve You with wholehearted devotion and a willing mind? I submit myself to You—I surrender my will to Yours (Psalm 139:23, 19:14; Deuteronomy 6:5; 1 Samuel 12:24; 1 Chronicles 28:9; James 4:7; Luke 22:42).

paths of Gold: A Month of prayers for a Lost friend

By Terry Gooding

We all have family, friends, and neighbors who have not come to a saving knowledge of God's grace. They do not know Jesus as their Savior. Our hearts are burdened when we know our loved ones are missing the best God has for them.

The Lord once gave me a word picture for encouragement as I began to grow weary in praying for an unsaved family member. I saw a picture in my mind that each prayer we pray is like placing a gold brick in our loved one's path. Our prayers are paving a golden road from earth to the throne room of heaven.

I pray these Scripture prayers will be helpful as you are praying for your friends and family. May the Lord give you the certainty to know you are asking according to His will because He desires "all men to be saved and to come to a knowledge of the truth" (1 Timothy 2:4). May the Lord bless you with perseverance as you offer each golden prayer.

1. May _____ know that he/she cannot stand on his/her own righteousness. No one can because there is no one righteous, not even one (Romans 3:10).

2. Although _____ has been spiritually blind, please give him/her eyes to see Jesus (John 9:25).

3. May _____ know You are Lord; and there is no Savior besides You (Isaiah 43:11).

4. Lord, may _____ know that You desire for him/her to be saved and come to the knowledge of Your truth (1 Timothy 2:4).

5. Open _____'s eyes and help him/her to turn from darkness and receive forgiveness of sins (Acts 26:18).

6. Help _____ to know that he/she can receive deliverance from the kingdom of darkness and step into the kingdom of Jesus (Colossians 1:13).

7. Lord, I pray that Satan will no longer blind _____'s mind, which causes him/her not to believe and to be unable to see the light of the gospel of Christ (2 Corinthians 4:4).

8. As _____ begins to hear Your voice, may he/she not harden his/her heart (Psalm 95:7-8).

9. Lord, please direct _____'s heart into Your love and into the steadfastness of Christ (2 Thessalonians 3:5).

10. Give a new heart to _____ that he/she may know You and receive You as his/her Lord and Savior (Jeremiah 24:7).

11. Plow up the hardened heart of _____ so that it can become good soil to hear the Word and bear fruit (Matthew 13:8).

12. Remove the heart of stone from _____, and give him/her a new heart of flesh (Ezekiel 11:19).

13. Jesus, I pray _____ will be pierced to the heart when he/she hears the good news about You (Acts 2:37).

14. May _____ know his/her sins have caused a separation between him/her and You, God (Isaiah 59:2).

15. Father, I pray _____ will know You have declared that all men/women should repent (Acts 17:30).

16. I ask that _____ know how patient You are toward him/her and that You do not wish for him/her to perish but to come to repentance (2 Peter 3:9).

17. Help _____ to understand that he/she can have forgiveness through the blood of Christ (Ephesians 1:7).

18. I pray _____ will confess his/her sins so that he/she can experience Your faithfulness to forgive sin and to cleanse from all unrighteousness (1 John 1:9).

19. Lord, would You gently instruct _____ and grant _____ repentance and a knowledge of the truth (2 Timothy 2:25)?

20. Father, produce a godly sorrow in _____, which will bring about repentance that leads to salvation and leaves no regrets (2 Corinthians 7:10).

21. May _____ understand that he/she can be saved by grace and that it is a free gift from You (Ephesians 2:8).

22. Jesus, may _____ know that Yours is the only name under heaven by which he/she can be saved (Acts 4:12).

23. Give _____ wisdom that leads to salvation through faith in Christ Jesus (2 Timothy 3:15).

24. Father God, I pray _____ will confess Jesus as Lord and believe that You raised Him from the dead, which will result in his/her salvation (Romans 10:9).

25. Father, I pray _____ will repent, be baptized in the name of Jesus, and receive the gift of the Holy Spirit (Acts 2:38).

26. Lord, help _____ to know how much You love him/her even though he/she is a sinner. Cause _____ to realize that You sent Your Son, Jesus Christ, to die for his/her sin (Romans 5:8).

27. I pray that the gospel would be presented to _____, not only with words, but also with power and with the Holy Spirit and deep conviction (1 Thessalonians 1:5).

28. Father, please send a faithful witness who can go to _____ and preach the gospel (Mark 16:15).

29. I ask You, Lord of the Harvest, to send out workers to surround _____ with the Word of God (Matthew 9:38).

30. Teach me to make the most of every opportunity I have to share the gospel with _____ (Colossians 4:5).

31. Help me to be the fragrance of Christ when I am with _____ (2 Corinthians 2:15).

TERRY GOODING is a prayer leader from El Paso, Texas. This article is adapted from *Paths of Gold: Praying the Way to Christ for Lost Friends and Family.* (*Pray!* Books) © 2002 by Terry Gooding. To order this article call 1-800-366-7788, or go to www.praymag.com. It is available both as an expanded version in a booklet (1-57683-396-8) or as a perpetual calendar (1-57683-629-0).

April

casting your cares

"Granted, God's answer might be found by seeking advice from a friend or waiting for the difficulty to take care of itself. But it is a waste of time to pursue any course of action until God has specifically directed us to do so. Prayer first, not last, is always the best course of action."

—Tom Elliff

Tom Elliff, *A Passion for Prayer* (Wheaton, IL: Crossway Books, 1998), p. 74.

> **Do not be anxious about anything,** but in everything, by prayer and petition, with thanksgiving, present your requests to God. And the peace of God, which transcends all understanding, will guard your hearts and your minds in Christ Jesus.
>
> —Philippians 4:6,7

APRIL 1 · Deuteronomy 27–30, Psalm 48

APRIL 2 · Deuteronomy 31–34, Psalm 49

APRIL 3 · James 1–2, Psalm 50

Lighten the Load

Have you ever carried a heavy briefcase, purse, or backpack, full of all the "stuff" you need for the day? Sometimes we also carry heavy loads of feelings,

April 4 · James 3-5, Psalm 51

April 5 · Joshua 1-3, Psalm 52

April 6 · Joshua 4-6, Psalm 53

troubles, and worries, and it saps our energy and joy.

God wants you to know that it's okay to bring all those feelings and needs to Him. You can pour out your heart—everything you are feeling! You can tell Him your needs—all of them! You don't have to put on a happy face when you pray. You can tell God even when you're really angry, afraid, or sad.

So lighten the load! Petition God for His help, and two great things happen. His peace will fill your heart and de-stress your mind. And your petition will pave the way for God to work out an answer to your situation.

—Cheri Fuller
(*Pray*Kids!, pp. 1-2, *Pray!* Issue 37, pp. 25-26.)

> "This, then, is how you should pray: 'Our Father in heaven, hallowed be your name, your kingdom come, your will be done on earth as it is in heaven. Give us today our daily bread. Forgive us our debts, as we also have forgiven our debtors. And lead us not into temptation, but deliver us from the evil one.'"
>
> —Matthew 6:9-13

APRIL 7 · *Reflection*

APRIL 8 · Joshua 7-9, Psalm 54

APRIL 9 · Joshua 10-12, Psalm 55

HOW TO PRAY?

Of the six commands in the Lord's Prayer, five relate to spiritual needs, and one is for physical needs. Does this ratio hold true in your own prayer life?

APRIL 10 · Joshua 13-15, Psalm 56

APRIL 11 · Joshua 16-18, Psalm 57

APRIL 12 · Joshua 19-21, Psalm 58

Unfortunately, Christians often spend far too much time praying for things: money, jobs, houses, cars. Too seldom do we pray for our spiritual needs: attitudes, emotions, our ability to trust Him, our desire to be more like Him.

God is interested in your physical needs and you should bring them up to Him! But He has already promised to meet the physical needs of those who walk with Him (Matthew 6:25-34; Philippians 4:19). Bringing these requests to Him is good for us, reminding us of our dependence on Him. But the emphasis in the New Testament is on spiritual needs, those areas that have eternal significance.

—Will Wyatt
(*Discovery: God's Answers to Our Deepest Questions*, Dawson Media, © 2001. Used with permission.)

> **Cast your cares** on the LORD and he will sustain you; he will never let the righteous fall.
>
> —Psalm 55:22

"I can't pray"

Sometimes it's not that we don't want to pray—it's that we cannot pray. What then? Here are some suggestions for breaking through when we find it difficult to pray.

• Keep trying. Don't give up—that's just what the enemy wants! Say the words, even if the feelings aren't there.

• Sing hymns that express the way you feel—or want to feel.

APRIL 13 · Joshua 22-24, Psalm 59

APRIL 14 · *Reflection*

APRIL 15 · Matthew 1-4, Psalm 60

April 16 · Matthew 5-7, Psalm 61

April 17 · Matthew 8-10, Psalm 62

April 18 · Matthew 11-13, Psalm 63

• Rest on promises. Use your Bible concordance to discover promises that will help you in your present circumstances. Personalize them by inserting your name.

• Cry to God. Are your prayers choked by tears? Sometimes weeping is praying. Paul says the Spirit intercedes for us when we cannot pray—with groans that words cannot express (Romans 8:26).

• Share your burden. Sometimes the burden is just too heavy for one person. Go to a trusted friend and say, "I can't pray. Will you pray for me?"

—Cynthia Hyle Bezek
(*Pray!*, Issue 14, p. 24.)

As she kept on praying to the LORD, Eli observed her mouth. Hannah was praying in her heart, and her lips were moving but her voice was not heard. Eli thought she was drunk and said to her, "How long will you keep on getting drunk? Get rid of your wine." "Not so, my lord," Hannah replied, "I am a woman who is deeply troubled. I have not been drinking wine or beer; I was pouring out my soul to the LORD. Do not take your servant for a wicked woman; I have been praying here out of my great anguish and grief."

—1 Samuel 1:12-16

APRIL 19 · Matthew 14-16, Psalm 64

APRIL 20 · Matthew 17-19, Psalm 65

APRIL 21 · *Reflection*

APRIL 22 · Matthew 20-22, Psalm 66

APRIL 23 · Matthew 23-25, Psalm 67

APRIL 24 · Matthew 26-28, Psalm 68

why do you ask?

God wants us to share our deepest desires with Him, just as Hannah did (see 1 Samuel 1:12-16). Sometimes, though, we find out that we are asking for the wrong reasons. This happened to two of Jesus' disciples.

James and John came to Jesus one day saying, "Teacher . . . we want you to do for us whatever we ask" (Mark 10:35). Then they asked Him to give them seats of honor right next to His throne when they got to heaven!

Jesus didn't scold them for making such a self-centered request. But He did tell them that they didn't understand what they were asking. He explained that those special seats would be given to people who suffered greatly for Him.

Go ahead and ask God anything that is important to you. Take time to think through why you are asking. Are your petitions self-serving or God-honoring?
—Cynthia Bezek
(Adapted from *Pray*Kids!, p. 2, *Pray!*, Issue 37, p. 29.)

> "So do not worry, saying, 'What shall we eat?' or 'What shall we drink?' or 'What shall we wear?' For the pagans run after all these things, and your heavenly Father knows that you need them. But seek first his kingdom and his righteousness, and all these things will be given to you as well."
>
> —Matthew 6:31-33

DAILY BREAD & PEANUT BUTTER

In my college days, things were pretty tight and we did a lot of asking of the Lord for daily provision. In addition to my studies, I was working a part-time job and actively involved in

APRIL 25 • Judges 1-3, Psalm 69:1-18

APRIL 26 • Judges 4-6, Psalm 69:19-36

APRIL 27 • Judges 7-9, Psalm 70

APRIL 28 · Judges 10-12, Psalm 71

APRIL 29 · *Reflection*

APRIL 30 · *Reflection*

ministry, and my wife, Nancy, was having our third child. We loved the Lord and each other but were as poor as dirt!

As we prayed, though, God supplied our needs in extraordinary ways. A friend sold us a nearly new Volvo for $1. Another person handed us a check to cover the total cost of our third child, as we were without health insurance. But my favorite happened one day when I was in class.

Nancy and our two-year-old Joy heard some rustling at the front door. When they peeked through the curtains, they saw the whole porch was filled with bags of groceries. As Nancy and Joy plucked each item out of the bags, little Joy beamed with excitement as she exclaimed, "Look, Mommy, Jesus gave us peanut butter!"

—Bill Teten
The Navigators

Notes

_____
_____
_____
_____
_____
_____
_____
_____
_____
_____

Monthly Reflection

What is the Spirit of God saying to me this month? What is my response?

_____
_____
_____
_____
_____
_____
_____
_____
_____
_____

Prayer for the Month:

Father, I cast all my cares on You—I know You will sustain me and never let me fall. I place every anxious thought at Your feet because You care for me. Instead of anxiety, I choose to come to You with my requests and a heart full of thanks. I know that worry can't accomplish anything, so I choose to bring You all my weariness and every burden. I receive Your rest. Thank You for Your grace—it is sufficient. I rely on Your strength, which is perfect in my weakness (Psalm 55:22; 1 Peter 5:7; Philippians 4:6; Luke 12:25; Matthew 11:28; 2 Corinthians 12:9).

31 ways to praise

By Bob Hostetler

I'm not often at a loss for words. My wife says that when we first began dating, the words I used to describe her considerable charms were partly responsible for her budding love for me. Later, as a pastor and preacher, I seldom struggled to find something to say, either in or out of the pulpit. And, of course, as a writer, my longtime friendship with words has stood me in good stead (after all, writers are often paid by the word!).

I've always been able to hold up my end of a conversation without difficulty. Except, that is, when it came to prayer, and particularly when I tried to express my praise to God. Attempting to begin and end my prayer times with praise and adoration, I often found myself flat-out speechless. I wanted to praise God with all that was within me, but I couldn't think of one sensible thing to say.

I recently read a book called *Invading the Privacy of God* by Cecil "Cec" Murphey. The book describes how Cec's prayer life was revolutionized when he settled on the practice of praying God's attributes as praise. I began imitating that practice in my own times of praise, and over the course of a few months, I developed a "program of praise" that has proven wonderfully helpful. It has opened a door for me, and my praises to God now flow freely from my heart and lips during prayer. I focus on one attribute of my awesome God and Father each day, using the Scripture-based sentences as "praise starters." At the end of each month, I start the list over, combining traits when the month is shorter than 31 days.

1. **God the Creator.** "Creator God, I praise You because 'you made the heavens, even the highest heavens, and all their starry host, the earth and all that is on it, the seas and all that is in them. You give life to everything, and the multitudes of heaven worship you'" (Nehemiah 9:6).

2. **The Only God.** "God, I praise You because You are 'the LORD, and there is no other; apart from [You] there is no God'" (Isaiah 45:5).

3. **The Almighty God.** "'O LORD God Almighty, who is like you? You are mighty, O LORD, and your faithfulness surrounds you'" (Psalm 89:8).

4. **The Everlasting Father, the Ancient of Days.** "I praise You, Lord, as the 'Ancient of Days' (Daniel 7:9), the 'Everlasting Father' (Isaiah 9:6), who lives forever and ever."

5. **A Loving God.** "I praise You because You are a loving God, whose very nature is love" (1 John 4:16).

6. **A God of Justice.** "Lord, I praise You and magnify You, who is 'just and the one who justifies those who have faith

in Jesus'" (Romans 3:26).

7. **A Faithful God.** "Heavenly Father, I give You my praise and adoration, because You are a 'faithful God, keeping [Your] covenant of love to a thousand generations of those who love [You] and keep [Your] commands'" (Deuteronomy 7:9).

8. **A Merciful God.** "'You are a gracious and merciful God' (Nehemiah 9:31), and I praise You for Your great mercy."

9. **God, My Refuge, My Fortress.** "I praise You, Lord, for You are 'my mighty rock, my refuge'" (Psalm 62:7).

10. **A Patient, Persevering God.** "Father, I praise You because You are 'patient with [Your children], not wanting anyone to perish, but everyone to come to repentance' (2 Peter 3:9). Thank You for Your patience with me."

11. **Eternal, Saving God.** "I give praise to You, Father, 'the only God our Savior.' To You 'be glory, majesty, power and authority, through Jesus Christ our Lord, before all ages, now and forevermore'" (Jude 25).

12. The Holy One. "Holy, holy, holy [are You] Lord God Almighty, who was, and is, and is to come" (Revelation 4:8).

13. A Personal God. "I praise You, God, because You are a personal God, who gives me the honor of knowing You personally, even inviting me to feast at Your kingdom's table with Abraham, Isaac, and Jacob" (Matthew 8:11).

14. A Giving God. "All praise and honor be Yours, O God, because You are a generous God, who did not even stop short of giving Your own Son" (John 3:16).

15. A Provider God. "I praise You today, Lord, as my Jehovah-Jireh (the Lord Will Provide), who makes all grace abound in me and generously provides all I need" (2 Corinthians 9:8).

16. God, My Shepherd. "I bless Your name and praise You as my Jehovah-Rohi (The Lord My Shepherd), who will shepherd me and guide me in the paths of righteousness for Your name's sake" (Psalm 23:1-3).

17. God, My Victory. "Praise to You, my God, because You are my Jehovah-Nissi (The Lord My Banner), God, my victory, 'who always leads [me] in triumphal procession in Christ'" (2 Corinthians 2:14).

18. God, My Peace. "I praise You with all my heart, Lord, because You are my Jehovah-Shalom (The Lord Our Peace), 'the God of peace [who] will soon crush Satan under [my] feet'" (Romans 16:20).

19. The God Who Heals. "Father, I praise You because You are the Lord who heals me" (Ezekiel 15:26).

20. The God of All Comfort. "Praise be to the God and Father of our Lord Jesus Christ, the Father of compassion and the God of all comfort" (2 Corinthians 1:3).

21. The God of Miracles. "Lord, I praise You because 'you are the God who performs miracles; you display your power among the peoples'" (Psalm 77:14).

22. A Forgiving God. "I want to bless You with praise, Father, because 'you are a forgiving God, gracious and compassionate, slow to anger and abounding in love'" (Nehemiah 9:17).

23. The Burden Bearer. "Praise be to the Lord, to God [my] Savior, who daily bears [my] burdens" (Psalm 68:19).

24. A Faithful God. "I praise You because 'your love, O LORD, reaches to the heavens, your faithfulness to the skies' (Psalm 36:5), and 'great is your faithfulness'" (Lamentations 3:23).

25. King of Kings and Lord of Lords. "All honor and praise be to You, my God, 'the blessed and only Ruler, the King of kings and Lord of lords, who alone is immortal and who lives in unapproachable light'" (1 Timothy 6:15-16).

26. God the Liberator. "I will praise You because 'you are my help and my deliverer; O LORD'" (Psalm 70:5).

27. The Lifter of My Head. "Father God, I praise You because 'you are a shield around me, O LORD; you bestow glory on me and lift up my head' when I am weary or despised" (Psalm 3:3).

28. God of Light. "I praise You, Lord, because You are 'my light and my salvation' (Psalm 27:1), and because You know 'what lies in darkness, and light dwells with [You]'" (Daniel 2:22).

29. God of Joy. "I give You praise, O Lord, because 'you have granted [me] eternal blessings and made [me] glad with the joy of your presence'" (Psalm 21:6).

30. The God Who Answers Prayer. "I praise and honor You, Father, because You are a God who loves to answer prayer and who begins to answer even before I pray" (Isaiah 65:24).

31. The God of All the Earth. "I praise and adore You, Lord, as 'the Holy One of Israel . . . [my] Redeemer . . . the God of all the earth'" (Isaiah 54:5).

Following this "praise program" has energized my praise life, helping me to worship and adore God more plentifully and purposefully in prayer. It has also enlarged my vision and awareness of the praiseworthy God I love and serve and, I believe, increased the evidence of His godly character in my life. I pray that it may do the same for you.

BOB HOSTETLER is an award-winning author of 12 books, including *Don't Leave Your Brains at the Door* (coauthored with Josh McDowell). This article is taken from *Pray!*, Issue 12, pp. 23. To order this article as a full-color bookmark prayer guide (50 per pack), call 1-800-366-7788 and ask for item #248 or go to www.navpress.com.

May

praying for others

"By the same work of the Spirit within us, I believe we can learn to look beyond our personal situation to those around us— our families, our communities, our nation, and our world. God will instill His concern for others within our hearts so that we can start to care for them as He does. Our prayers for them begin to flow more readily. We yearn for others to receive their salvation from His hand, to know His tender care as their Father and Friend."

—Shirley Dobson

Shirley Dobson, *Certain Peace in Uncertain Times* (Sisters, OR: Multnomah Publishers, Inc., 2002), p. 43.

> **Jesus went through all the towns and villages,** teaching in their synagogues, preaching the good news of the kingdom and healing every disease and sickness. When he saw the crowds, he had compassion on them, because they were harassed and helpless, like sheep without a shepherd. Then he said to his disciples, "The harvest is plentiful but the workers are few. Ask the Lord of the harvest, therefore, to send out workers into his harvest field."
>
> —Matthew 9:35-38

May 1 · Judges 13-15, Proverbs 18

May 2 · Judges 16-18, Proverbs 19:1-14

May 3 · Judges 19-21, Proverbs 19:15-29

MAY 4 · Romans 1-3, Proverbs 20:1-15

MAY 5 · Romans 4-5, Proverbs 20:16-30

MAY 6 · Romans 6-8, Proverbs 21:1-16

pray for the crowds

Prayer warriors can identify with Jesus' heart of compassion for the crowds. Perhaps you've felt there are so many needs and so little time to pray. Here are some tips to help you maximize your prayer time for the needy "crowds" in your life:

• *Pray now.* If someone calls or approaches you with a need, stop and pray right then.

• *Pray simply.* A simple, sincere prayer can unleash the power of God like a keg of dynamite in the heavenlies.

• *Pray always.* Though God may call you to seasons of protracted intercession from time to time, every day can be filled with exciting prayer moments.

• *Pray intentionally.* Place pictures of missionaries on your refrigerator or in your prayer journal. Slip a country's name in your wallet, and pray whenever you open it.

—Tricia McCary Rhodes
(*Pray!*, Issue 8, p. 35.)

> "Teacher, which is the greatest commandment in the Law?" Jesus replied: "'Love the Lord your God with all your heart and with all your soul and with all your mind.' This is the first and greatest commandment. And the second is like it: 'Love your neighbor as yourself.'"
>
> —Matthew 22:36-39

MAY 7 · *Reflection*

MAY 8 · Romans 9-11, Proverbs 21:17-31

MAY 9 · Romans 12-13, Proverbs 22:1-16

PRAY for the Neighborhood

Want to get serious about loving your neighbors as yourself? Here are several ways you can pray for your neighborhood.

may 10 · Romans 14-16, Proverbs 22:17-29

may 11 · Ruth, Proverbs 23:1-18

may 12 · Ephesians 1-3, Proverbs 23:19-35

• Draw a sketch of your neighborhood or print one from the Internet. Mark house numbers and the names of neighbors you know. Add others as you meet them. Record any specific issues that you either know or sense may need God's intervention.

• Pray regularly for each household, that their eyes would be opened to the existence and power of God, and that their hearts would be softened toward Him. Pray for their protection and release from the schemes of the evil one against them.

• Take walks in your community. Pray as you go through the streets you've mapped. Pray for people by name as you walk by their house. Intercede for the needs you have noticed. Ask the Holy Spirit to make you sensitive to any other issues that may need your prayer.

—Arlyn Lawrence
(*Pray!*, Issue 35, p. 40.)

> As [Jesus] **approached Jerusalem** and saw the city, he wept over it and said, "If you, even you, had only known on this day what would bring you peace—but now it is hidden from your eyes."
>
> —Luke 19:41,42

May 13 · Ephesians 4-6, Proverbs 24:1-22

May 14 · *Reflection*

Pray for the cities

Jesus wept over Jerusalem. Just as biblical prophets such as Daniel, Jeremiah, Nehemiah, and Paul did, believers in our day need to intercede for our cities. Here are four prayers to get you started:

1. Pray for all God's people to get God's heart for the city. As God's

May 15 · 1 Samuel 1-3, Proverbs 24:23-34

May 16 · 1 Samuel 4-6, Proverbs 25:1-14

May 17 · 1 Samuel 7-9, Proverbs 25:15-28

May 18 · 1 Samuel 10-12, Proverbs 26:1-16

people gain His broken heart for cities, particularly for the poor, their prayers will be powerful agents for change.

2. Pray with understanding for specific aspects of your city. Missionaries know that it's ineffective to enter a culture without first understanding its traditions and history. Do your homework and foster understanding in your prayers.

3. Pray against stereotypes and misconceptions. Every city has many needs: A CEO of a huge corporation, for instance, is as much in need of prayer for purpose in his or her life as a homeless family.

4. Pray consistently for churches and faith-based ministries in the cities. Pastors and layleaders are working tirelessly in cities to bring the good news of Jesus Christ to the people in their communities. Pray for them!

—Jo Kadlecek
(*Pray!*, Issue 6, pp. 26-31.)

> **And pray in the Spirit** on all occasions with all kinds of prayers and requests. With this in mind, be alert and always keep on praying for all the saints. Pray also for me, that whenever I open my mouth, words may be given me so that I will fearlessly make known the mystery of the gospel, for which I am an ambassador in chains. Pray that I may declare it fearlessly, as I should.
>
> —Ephesians 6:18-20

pray for missionaries

In his various writings, the apostle Paul—the first great

may 19 · 1 Samuel 13-15, Proverbs 26:17-28

may 20 · 1 Samuel 16-19, Proverbs 27:1-14

may 21 · *Reflection*

MAY 22 · 1 Samuel 20-22, Proverbs 27:15-27

MAY 23 · 1 Samuel 23-25, Proverbs 28:1-14

MAY 24 · 1 Samuel 26-28, Proverbs 28:15-28

missionary—gives present-day followers of Christ at least six ways to pray for missionaries:

1. *Acceptance* by other missionaries, each focused and called by God, but at times with different ideas about how to reach a particular group of people (Romans 15:31).

2. *Boldness* when it comes to presenting the good news (Ephesians 6:19).

3. *Clarity* to communicate the gospel clearly, so that the message is clearly understood despite any communication barriers (Colossians 4:4).

4. *Deliverance* from the attack of the enemy, from whatever direction the attack may come (Romans 15:31).

5. *Extension* so that the ministry may be extended beyond its current boundaries (Colossians 4:3).

6. *Fruitfulness*, that the gospel is spread, accepted, and takes root (2 Thessalonians 3:1).

—Dave Butts

(*Pray!*, Issue 1, p. 25.)

write an encouraging prayer

How often have you heard or said these words: "I'll pray for you" or "You'll be in my prayers"? They're said so easily, yet so often they sound unconvincing.

May 25 · 1 Samuel 29-31, Proverbs 29:1-14

May 26 · Philippians, Proverbs 29:15-27

May 27 · 2 Samuel 1-3, Proverbs 30

MAY 28 · 2 Samuel 4-7, Proverbs 31

MAY 29 · *Reflection*

MAY 30 · *Reflection*

For some, they are an easy way to end a conversation. How many times are these words actually acted upon?

A good way to let the people you're praying for know that you really are praying is to write out the prayer on a greeting card or stationery, with a note that says, "I offered this prayer for you today." If the person you're praying for has email, send the prayer that way.

When you write out prayers for others, you tell them that you really believe in prayer, that you understand their needs, and that you're concerned about them. Keep a copy of the prayers as reminders to keep on praying!

—Willard A. Scofield
(*Pray!*, Issue 13, p. 7.)

may 31 · *Reflection*

_____
_____
_____
_____
_____
_____
_____
_____
_____
_____
_____

monthly reflection

What is the Spirit of God saying to me this month? What is my response?

_____
_____
_____
_____
_____
_____
_____
_____
_____
_____

prayer for the month:

Thank You, Father, for the incredible privilege of partnering with Jesus in the work of intercession. Help me to stay alert and consistent as I pray for my brothers and sisters in Christ. Help me be clear minded and self-controlled as I stand in the gap for others, especially during these times. Remind me that prayerlessness for others is sin against You. Help me be instant in prayer so that it becomes a way of life for me, as continuous as breathing (Hebrews 7:25; Ephesians 6:18; 1 Peter 4:7; Ezekiel 22:30; 1 Samuel 12:23; Romans 12:12; 1 Thessalonians 5:17).

30 ways to pray for people in authority

By Gary P. Bergel

The life of every citizen of every nation is impacted by a vast multitude of individuals who wield significant influence each day. Consider: millions of elected officials, appointed judges, lawyers, police officers, bureaucrats, military officers, business executives and managers, those involved in church leadership, educators, medical practitioners and hospital administrators. How might we pray for these individuals? Here are 30 things based on Scripture that we can pray for people in authority. Don't overwhelm yourself. Select one person or group of people and then pray one of these things each day for them.

1. That they be God-fearing and recognize that they are accountable to Him for each decision and act (Proverbs 9:10).

2. That they be granted wisdom, knowledge, and understanding (James 1:5).

3. That they be presented with the gospel and a loving Christian witness (Romans 10:14-15).

4. That, if unsaved, they be drawn to a saving encounter with Christ; that, if born again, they be strengthened and encouraged in their faith (1 Timothy 2:4; Ephesians 1:17-23).

5. That they recognize their own inadequacy and pray and seek the will of God (Proverbs 3:5-8; Luke 11:9-13).

6. That they be convicted of sin, transgression, and iniquity (Psalm 51:17; John 8:9).

7. That they heed their conscience, confess their sins, and repent (Proverbs 28:13; James 4:8).

8. That they read the Bible and attend prayer meetings and Bible studies (Psalm 119:11; Colossians 3:2).

9. That they value and regard the Ten Commandments and the teachings of Christ (Psalm 19:7-11; John 8:31-32).

10. That they respect and honor their parents (Ephesians 6:2-3).

11. That they respect authority and practice accountability (Romans 13:1-7).

12. That they be given godly counsel and God-fearing advisors (Proverbs 24:6).

13. That they be honest and faithful to spouses and children (Malachi 2:15-16).

14. That they be practicing members of local congregations (Hebrews 10:25).

15. That they desire purity and avoid debauchery, pornography, perversion, and drunkenness (1 Corinthians 6:9-20; Titus 2:12).

16. That they be timely, reliable, and dependable (Matthew 21:28-31).

17. That they be honest in financial, tax, and ethical matters (1 Corinthians 6:10; 1 Timothy 6:6-10).

18. That they seek pastoral care and counsel when needed (Hebrews 13:7).

19. That they seek out and nurture godly friendships (Psalm 1:1-3).

20. That they have thankful and teachable spirits (Romans 1:21).

21. That they be generous and have compassionate hearts

for the poor and needy (Psalm 112:9; Luke 10:33-37).

22. That they redeem their time and know their priorities (Ephesians 5:15-17).

23. That they desire honesty, integrity, and loyalty (Psalm 26; Proverbs 11:3).

24. That they have courage to resist manipulation, pressure, and the fear of man (Proverbs 29:25; 2 Timothy 1:7).

25. That they be shielded from occultism, New Age cults, false religions, and secret societies (Isaiah 1:29, 2:6).

26. That they be presented with biblical worldviews and principles (Ephesians 3:10).

27. That they endeavor to restore the sanctity of life, families, divine order, and morality in our nation (Ephesians 5:21-6:4).

28. That they would work to reverse the trends of humanism in our nation (1 Chronicles 12:32; Isaiah 59:19).

29. That they desire humility and meekness and be willing to serve and cooperate (John 13:14, Titus 3:1-2).

30. That they be prepared to give account to Almighty God (Hebrews 9:27).

GARY P. BERGEL is the president of Intercessors for America (www.ifa-usapray.org), an organization that provides intercessors with factual information to fuel their prayers for government. This article is taken from *Pray!*, Issue 13, p. 7. To order this article as a full-color bookmark prayer guide (50 per pack), call 1-800-366-7788 and ask for item #246, or go to www.praymag.com.

June

asking in Faith

"Sometimes we are afraid that we do not have enough faith to pray for this child or that marriage. Our fears should be put to rest, for the Bible tells us that great miracles are possible through faith the size of a tiny mustard seed. Usually the courage actually to go and pray for a person is a sign of sufficient faith."

—Richard J. Foster

Richard J. Foster, *Celebration of Discipline* (San Francisco, CA: Harper & Row, 1978), p. 35.

This is the confidence we have in approaching God: that if we ask anything according to his will, he hears us. And if we know that he hears us—whatever we ask—we know that we have what we asked of him.

—1 John 5:14,15

without a doubt

Though the last penny was spent and the cupboards remained bare, the small group gathered confidently around the table and bowed their heads in thanksgiving. The "amen" had barely escaped their lips when

JUNE 1 · 2 Samuel 8-10, Psalm 72

JUNE 2 · 2 Samuel 11-13, Psalm 73

JUNE 3 · 2 Samuel 14-17, Psalm 74

June 4 · 2 Samuel 18-20, Psalm 75

June 5 · 2 Samuel 21-24, Psalm 76

June 6 · Colossians, Psalm 77

the doorbell sounded. There a man stood, arms full of food. He just had felt an urge to stop by. I'd read many similar accounts in the biographies of great Christians. Godly men and women who believed their God, asked Him boldly, and received their requests. And then there was me. It's not that I thought God *couldn't* answer my prayers. It's just that I wasn't so sure that He'd *want* to.

In recent years I've come to see that my doubts were hindering my prayers, and that I needed to confess—not ignore, rationalize, or hide—my doubt. As I make this more and more of a practice, the Lord is opening my eyes to the many ways He is working around me every day!

—Angela Spitzer
(*Pray!*, Issue 18, pp. 31-32.)

> **"Is anything too hard for the LORD?** I will return to you at the appointed time next year and Sarah will have a son."
>
> —Genesis 18:14

june 7 · *Reflection*

june 8 · 1 Kings 1-3, Psalm 78:1-39

god is able

"And the prayer offered in faith will make the sick person well," says James, an early church leader and half-brother of Jesus, "the Lord will raise him up. If he has sinned, he will be forgiven" (James 5:15).

James indicates that the prayer offered in faith will be answered, so it's important that

june 9 · 1 Kings 4-6, Psalm 78:40-72

JUNE 10 · 1 Kings 7-9, Psalm 79

JUNE 11 · 1 Kings 10-12, Psalm 80

JUNE 12 · 1 Kings 13-15, Psalm 81

we know in our heart of hearts that God does indeed hear and can answer any prayer. We need the confidence expressed in Genesis 18:14, that *nothing* is too difficult for the Lord! God is *able* to do anything that He has promised to do because He is:

• *omniscient*, able to know all things.

• *omnipotent*, able to do all things.

• *omnipresent*, able to be everywhere at the same time.

Beyond believing that God *can* answer, we must believe that the prayer offered in faith ensures He *will* answer—He will do so according to His will, which we learn from His Word.

—Elmer L. Towns
(*Pray!*, Issue 34, pp. 18-19.)

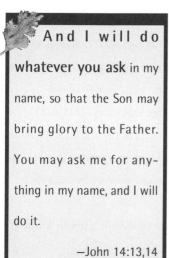

> **And I will do whatever you ask** in my name, so that the Son may bring glory to the Father. You may ask me for anything in my name, and I will do it.
>
> —John 14:13,14

June 13 · 1 Kings 16-19, Psalm 82

June 14 · *Reflection*

Road prayer-warriors

People on the highways always seem to be in a hurry and not always in the best of moods. Why not step out in faith, claim John 14:13-14, and bless those frantic travelers with prayer?

June 15 · 1 Kings 20-22, Psalm 83

June 16 · Jonah, Psalm 84

June 17 · Philemon, Psalm 85

June 18 · 2 Kings 1-4, Psalm 86

The idea came on a trip to Spokane, Washington. I'd just read our Bible selection as my husband, Don, pulled out of the motel parking lot. Glancing up, I saw a gray mini van. The words flew out of my mouth: "I bless you in the name of Jesus. Lord, help that mom. Have the kids settle down and be agreeable for the rest of her trip."

A wonderful revelation of God's grace flooded my heart. I began to pronounce the Lord's blessing on every driver on the freeway! Today I'm like a generous millionaire, lavishing God's love on countless people—and in faith I know God's responding!

—Elaine Hardt
(*Pray!*, Issue 3, p. 15.)

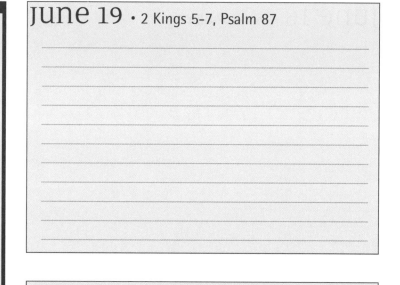

> Now to him who is able to do immea-surably more than all we ask or imagine, according to his power that is at work within us, to him be glory in the church and in Christ Jesus throughout all gener-ations, for ever and ever! Amen.
>
> —Ephesians 3:20,21

june 19 · 2 Kings 5-7, Psalm 87

june 20 · 2 Kings 8-11, Psalm 88

"Little" prayers?

Too often we miss what God is doing in a situation because we pray "little" prayers that focus on a narrow, specific outcome. The flesh prays little prayers.

june 21 · *Reflection*

June 22 · 2 Kings 12-14, Psalm 89:1-18

June 23 · 2 Kings 15-18, Psalm 89:19-52

June 24 · 2 Kings 19-21, Psalm 90

The flesh prays time-bound, earthbound prayers. "Flesh gives birth to flesh, but the Spirit gives birth to spirit" (John. 3:6).

God, however, commands us to "pray in the Spirit on all occasions with all kinds of prayers and requests" (Ephesians 6:18). The word translated "in" means "from a fixed position." Pray from your fixed position in the Spirit. Pray according to the mind of the Spirit, by the leading of the Spirit, in the power of the Spirit.

Prayer birthed by the Spirit releases the power of God to accomplish the purposes of God; and the power of God will do so much more than we can ask or imagine!

—Jennifer Kennedy Dean
(*Pray!*, Issue 31, p. 15.)

> **How gracious he will be** when you cry for help! As soon as he hears, he will answer you. Although the Lord gives you the bread of adversity and the water of affliction, your teachers will be hidden no more; with your own eyes you will see them. Whether you turn to the right or to the left, your ears will hear a voice behind you, saying, "This is the way; walk in it."
>
> —Isaiah 30:19-21

Pray Out Loud

A friend once told me how he'd felt deserted by everyone—his wife, children, friends, business

June 25 • 2 Kings 22-25, Psalm 91

June 26 • Luke 1-3, Psalm 92

June 27 • Luke 4-6, Psalm 93

June 28 · Luke 7-9, Psalm 94

June 29 · *Reflection*

June 30 · *Reflection*

associates. In the midst of that dark night, he turned to Isaiah 30. That night he audibly spoke to the Lord, praying back verses 19-21. And that's when he found the presence of the Lord in a new, closer way. He says that he had never felt the Lord's presence so closely, so intimately!

When you're feeling abandoned or lost, all it takes for God's grace to flood your soul is for Him to *hear your voice.* Why? Because God has committed Himself that when He hears your voice, He will answer you. Even in the midst of adversity and affliction, the Lord will evidence Himself through His presence.

The next time you feel alone, even abandoned, speak to the Lord in your heart and with your audible voice. Tell Him in detail how you feel. Ask for His presence. Submit your heart and will to His heart and will. Remember, He has committed Himself to be close and to speak to you when your heart and will, along with your voice, are in tune with Him.

—Lauren D. Libby
The Navigators

NOTES

MONTHLY REFLECTION

What is the Spirit of God saying to me this month? What is my response?

PRAYER FOR THE MONTH:

God, I approach You with freedom and confidence through faith in Jesus. I come eagerly desiring the spiritual gift of faith. Oh, how I want to please You by exercising my faith—You are almighty God, and You reward everyone who earnestly seeks You! I long to be single-minded and doubtless, offering prayers that heal the sick and move mountains (Ephesians 3:12; 1 Corinthians 14:1,12:9; Hebrews 11:6; James 1:6-8, 5:15; Matthew 17:20).

31 Biblical virtues to pray for your children

By Bob Hostetler

For years, like any responsible Christian parent, I prayed daily for my two children, Aubrey and Aaron. I prayed for God's blessing and protection throughout their days. I prayed for them to be happy. I asked God to help them through difficult times and to help them make wise choices. My prayers were regular, heartfelt, and—for the most part—pedestrian.

I wanted so much for my children. But when I knelt in prayer, I invariably found the same tired words rolling from my lips. Then one day, Nancy, our pastor's wife, shared a testimony during a morning worship service. She talked about her concern that her children develop strong Christian morals and the fruit of the Spirit. This had prompted her to develop a unique prayer list.

That day I decided to follow Nancy's example. I've developed a "parent's prayer program" of my own, a simple practice that has revolutionized the way I pray for my children. Each day of the month, in addition to my prayers for their safety and the concerns of that day, I also pray for a specific character trait, virtue, or fruit of the Spirit to be planted and nurtured in my children—through my efforts and my wife's, through the influence of others, and through Aubrey's and Aaron's own actions and decisions. At the end of each month, I begin praying through the list again, combining traits when the month is shorter than 31 days.

Following is my list, along with suggestions from Scripture. Feel free to duplicate it—or improve upon it—to help you pray specifically and purposefully for your own children.

1. **salvation.** "Lord, let salvation spring up within my children, that they may obtain the salvation that is in Christ Jesus, with eternal glory" (Isaiah 45:8; 2 Timothy 2:10).

2. **growth in grace.** "I pray that my children may grow in the grace and knowledge of our Lord and Savior Jesus Christ" (2 Peter 3:18).

3. **love.** "Grant, Lord, that my children may learn to live a life of love, through the Spirit who dwells in them" (Ephesians 5:2; Galatians 5:25).

4. **honesty and integrity.** "May integrity and honesty be their virtue and their protection" (Psalm 25:21).

5. **self-control.** "Father, help my children not to be like many others around them, but let them be alert and self-controlled in all they do" (1 Thessalonians 5:6).

6. **love for God's word.** "May my children grow to find Your Word more precious than much pure gold and sweeter than honey from the comb" (Psalm 19:10).

7. **justice.** "God, help my children to love justice as You do and act justly in all they do" (Psalm 11:7; Micah 6:8).

8. **mercy.** "May my children always be merciful, just as their Father is merciful" (Luke 6:36).

9. **respect (for self, others, authority).** "Father, grant that my children may show proper respect to everyone, as your Word commands" (1 Peter 2:17).

10. **biblical self-esteem.** "Help my children develop a strong self-esteem that is rooted in the realization that they are God's workmanship, created in Christ Jesus" (Ephesians 2:10).

11. **faithfulness.** "Let love and faithfulness never leave my children, but bind these twin virtues around their necks and write them on the tablet of their hearts" (Proverbs 3:3).

12. **courage.** "May my children always be strong and courageous in their character and in their actions" (Deuteronomy 31:6).

13. **purity.** "Create in them a pure heart, O God, and let that purity of heart be shown in their actions" (Psalm 51:10).

14. **kindness.** "Lord, may my children always try to be kind to each other and to everyone else" (1 Thessalonians 5:15).

15. **generosity.** "Grant that my children may be generous and willing to share, and so lay up treasure for themselves as a firm foundation for the coming age" (1 Timothy 6:18-19).

16. **peace-loving.** "Father, let my children make every effort to do what leads to peace" (Romans 14:19).

17. **joy.** "May my children be filled with the joy given by the Holy Spirit" (1 Thessalonians 1:6).

18. **perseverance.** "Lord, teach my children perseverance in all they do, and help them especially to run with perseverance the race marked out for them" (Hebrews 12:1).

19. **humility.** "God, please cultivate in my children the ability to show true humility toward all" (Titus 3:2).

20. **compassion.** "Lord, please clothe my children with the virtue of compassion" (Colossians 3:12).

21. **responsibility.** "Grant that my children may learn responsibility, for each one should carry his own load" (Galatians 6:5).

22. **contentment.** "Father, teach my children the secret of being content in any and every situation, through Him who gives them strength" (Philippians 4:12-13).

23. **faith.** "I pray that faith will find root and grow in my children's hearts, that by faith they may gain what has been promised to them" (Luke 17:5-6; Hebrews 11:1-40).

24. **A servant's heart.** "God, please help my children develop servants' hearts, that they may serve wholeheartedly, as if they were serving the Lord, not people" (Ephesians 6:7).

25. **hope.** "May the God of hope grant that my children may overflow with hope and hopefulness by the power of the Holy Spirit" (Romans 15:13).

26. **willingness and ability to work.** "Teach my children, Lord, to value work and to work at it with all their heart, as working for the Lord, not for men" (Colossians 3:23).

27. **passion for God.** "Lord, please instill in my children a soul that 'followeth hard after thee' (Psalm 63:8, KJV), one that clings passionately to You."

28. **self-discipline.** "Father, I pray that my children may acquire a disciplined and prudent life, doing what is right and just and fair" (Proverbs 1:3).

29. **prayerfulness.** "Grant, Lord, that my children's lives may be marked by prayerfulness, that they may learn to pray in the Spirit on all occasions with all kinds of prayers and requests" (Ephesians 6:18).

30. **gratitude.** "Help my children to live lives that are always overflowing with thankfulness and always giving thanks to God the Father for everything, in the name of our Lord Jesus Christ" (Colossians 2:7; Ephesians 5:20).

31. **A heart for missions.** "Lord, please help my children to develop a desire to see Your glory declared among the nations, Your marvelous deeds among all peoples" (Psalm 96:3).

After several weeks of praying through the above list for my children, I discovered an additional benefit to my prayer program: as I prayed with my children each night, the Lord brought to mind the subject I'd prayed for that morning, and I would repeat my request in Aubrey and Aaron's hearing. Before long, they began to echo my prayers, pouring out their own hearts in prayer for the virtues and qualities I desired to see in them. Thus, my simple prayer program has not only changed how I pray, but also how my children pray—and by God's grace, how we live as well.

BOB HOSTETLER lives near Oxford, Ohio, with his wife, Robin, and two children. This article is taken from *Pray!*, Issue 4, pp. 34-36. To order this article as a full-color bookmark prayer guide (50 per pack), call 1-800-366-7788, and ask for item #1051, or go to www.praymag.com.

july

waiting upon him

"[E]ven when God's people are praying just the right prayer about the concerns that God Himself has laid on their hearts, He still may keep them waiting, because the time He appoints for prayer-answering action is often not as soon as was hoped. So persistence in prayer, proving our seriousness of purpose as we keep our requests before the throne day after day, becomes a vital lesson that all God's people in every age need to learn."

—J. I. Packer

J. I. Packer, *A Passion for Faithfulness* (Wheaton, IL: Crossway Books, 1995), p. 63.

> "For my thoughts are not your thoughts, neither are your ways my ways," declares the LORD. "As the heavens are higher than the earth, so are my ways higher than your ways and my thoughts than your thoughts."
>
> —Isaiah 55:8-9

JULY 1 · Luke 10-12, Ecclesiastes 1

JULY 2 · Luke 13-15, Ecclesiastes 2:1-16

our purpose-driven God

Although our problems are forever changing, God's purposes remain constant. He ultimately will act according to those purposes:

JULY 3 · Luke 16-18, Ecclesiastes 2:17-26

JULY 4 · Luke 19-21, Ecclesiastes 3:1-15

JULY 5 · Luke 22-24, Ecclesiastes 3:16-22

JULY 6 · Amos 1-3, Ecclesiastes 4

• "But the plans of the LORD stand firm for ever, the purposes of his heart through all generations" (Psalm 33:11).

• "And we know that in all things God works for the good of those who love him, who have been called according to his purpose" (Romans 8:28).

It is in understanding God's purposes that we reach a higher level of prayer. God's answer to your problem today will be creative and it will be couched in His eternal purposes. Rest assured that anything God does for you in answer to prayer will be done in accordance with the glory of His name and the establishment of His kingdom.

—Eddie and Alice Smith
(*Pray!*, Issue 25, pp. 34-35.)

> **Even youths grow tired and weary**, and young men stumble and fall; but those who hope in the LORD will renew their strength. They will soar on wings like eagles; they will run and not grow weary, they will walk and not be faint.
>
> —Isaiah 40:30,31

7 waiting phases

There are seven phases of waiting on God. They are:

1. Intensity: A crisis causes you to focus all of your energy to pray for a divine solution.

2. Distraction: You cannot sustain indefinite intensity; your heart and mind are distracted.

JULY 7 · *Reflection*

JULY 8 · Amos 4-6, Ecclesiastes 5

JULY 9 · Amos 7-9, Ecclesiastes 6

JULY 10 · 1 Chronicles 1-4, Ecclesiastes 7:1-14

JULY 11 · 1 Chronicles 5-8, Ecclesiastes 7:15-29

JULY 12 · 1 Chronicles 9-11, Ecclesiastes 8

3. Anger: Anger emerges and is directed at God for not taking action, the cause of the problem, or yourself for not being able to do more.

4. Accusation: Satan the accuser says that God hasn't answered because of your sinfulness.

5. Frustration: You are no longer certain how to pray.

6. Revelation: Provided you stay in the Word, deeper understanding will develop about waiting on God for answered prayer.

7. Determination: Faith at this point is not a feeling, but a willful determination to be faithful in prayer, no matter how or when (if ever) God answers.

—Ron Susek

(*Pray!*, Issue 28, p. 18.)

> **Then Jesus told his disciples a parable** to show them that they should always pray and not give up. He said: "In a certain town there was a judge who neither feared God nor cared about men. And there was a widow in that town who kept coming to him with the plea, 'Grant me justice against my adversary.' For some time he refused. But finally he said to himself, 'Even though I don't fear God or care about men, yet because this widow keeps bothering me, I will see that she gets justice, so that she won't eventually wear me out with her coming!'"
>
> —Luke 18:1-5

JULY 13 · 1 Chronicles 12-14, Ecclesiastes 9

JULY 14 · *Reflection*

JULY 15 · 1 Chronicles 15-17, Ecclesiastes 10

JULY 16 · 1 Chronicles 18-20, Ecclesiastes 11

JULY 17 · 1 Chronicles 21-23, Ecclesiastes 12

JULY 18 · 1 Chronicles 24-26, Song of Songs 1

Delayed Response

Jesus' parable of the Persistent Widow encourages us to pray and not give up! Although God the Father is an obvious contrast to the godless judge, they have something in common: the choice to delay a response.

The judge delayed settling the widow's case out of selfish indifference. God often delays His response out of love, as He works all things together for good.

One of those "things" that needs to be worked out is the attitude of the one praying. God doesn't want whiny, demanding prayers. He wants humble and earnest asking, seeking, knocking. The very act of persisting in prayer can make us more worthy of His answer. We'll learn to praise Him as sovereign Lord.

—Jeanne Zornes
(*Pray!*, Issue 2, p. 30.)

JULY 19 · 1 Chronicles 27-29, Song of Songs 2

JULY 20 · Hosea 1-4, Song of Songs 3

JULY 21 · *Reflection*

no worries

When we are waiting for God to answer a prayer—especially over a long period of time—we can start to get worried. Yet Jesus

JULY 22 · Hosea 5-8, Song of Songs 4:1-7

JULY 23 · Hosea 9-11, Song of Songs 4:8-16

JULY 24 · Hosea 12-14, Song of Songs 5

tells us not to do so (see Matthew 6:25). So how can we avoid worry during the wait?

• Learn faith-building Scriptures to use when fear threatens to consume you.

• Let go of judgment and unforgiveness (see Mark 11:25).

• Don't give up. It's always too soon to stop praying.

• Don't dwell on the negatives; focus instead on the answer that is on the way (see Mark 11:23-24).

• Praise God, even before you see evidence of His intervention.

• Don't box God in with your own expectations or timetables.

• Cling to the Scriptures that comfort, committing them to memory.

—Quin Sherrer
and Ruthanne Gatlock
(*Pray!*, Issue 28, p. 32. Adapted from *Praying Prodigals Home* by Quin Sherrer and Ruthanne Gatlock [Regal Books], © 2000.)

> **Search me, O God,** and know my heart; test me and know my anxious thoughts. See if there is any offensive way in me, and lead me in the way everlasting.
>
> —Psalm 139:23,24

JULY 25 • 1 Corinthians 1-2, Song of Songs 6

JULY 26 • 1 Corinthians 3-5, Song of Songs 7

HAS GOD REPLIED?

You've made your requests known to God and are waiting for Him to reply. Perhaps He already has, but how can you know for sure? Take the following steps to find God's direction:

Pray: Ask God for confirmation in your heart. Pray about all aspects of what you are contemplating doing. Keep an open

JULY 27 • 1 Corinthians 6-8, Song of Songs 8:1-7

JULY 28 · 1 Corinthians 9-11, Song of Songs 8:8-14

JULY 29 · *Reflection*

JULY 30 · *Reflection*

mind to hear something else God might be telling you to do.

Read the Word: Go to God's Word and seek Him for a confirmation. It can come through God speaking through a passage and by a growing peace in your heart.

Study: If it is something you heard or read about that worked somewhere else, read everything you can on the subject. And don't be afraid to read something that might be critical of or have warnings about what you are considering. God can still confirm in your heart what He wants you to do.

Confirm through others: Have fellow believers pray with you about what you believe God is revealing. If God is leading you to do something, He will confirm it through others.

—Jon Graf

(*Pray!*, Issue 5, p. 4.)

JULY 31 · *Reflection*

montHLy RefLection

What is the Spirit of God saying to me this month? What is my response?

prayer for the montH:

My soul waits on You, O Lord—every expectation I have is from You. Renew my strength as I wait. I know the plans and purposes of Your heart stand firm. I choose to put my hope in Your Word as I wait. Even though there might be a delay before it's revealed, I know it is truth. Thank You for Your patience with me—I'm sorry when I misunderstand. I acknowledge that I can't even fathom the grand scope of what You're doing, but I know You make all things beautiful in Your perfect timing (Psalm 62:5; Isaiah 40:31; Psalms 33:11, 130:5; Habakkuk 2:3; 2 Peter 3:9; Ecclesiastes 3:11).

 21 Redemptive Prayers for Hollywood

By Larry Poland

Christians have attempted many strategies to reform the media/entertainment field. Separatism, avoidance, organized boycotts, and angry protests have failed to redeem the media.

Despite the extraordinary influence of filmmakers, TV producers, actors, and musicians worldwide, seldom are they and their industries prayed for. Each of these people is but one miracle away from a vital faith in God!

1. Father, thank You for the often unseen, positive influences of Christians in media. Protect them from growing tired or discouraged as they face negative challenges in their industry. Help them to be salt and light to those around them (Galatians 6:9; Matthew 5:13-14).

2. God of hope, fill Christians in media with contagious joy and peace that overflows in hope. Show them how to abide in You so that their exemplary lives have an eternal impact on co-workers (Romans 15:13; Matthew 5:15-16).

3. God, whenever Christians in media open their mouths, give them just the right words to share Your love without fear. Give them confidence to rely on Your help (Ephesians 6:19; Hebrews 13:6).

4. Lead Your people in media to be zealous and spiritually fervent as they serve You. Raise up godly men and women who will lead by example (Romans 12:11; 1 Corinthians 11:1).

5. Bless the homes of media professionals. Build their families on Your wisdom; establish them through understanding. Teach their children so that Your peace rules (Proverbs 3:33, 24:3; Isaiah 54:13).

6. Lord God, protect Christians in media from envy and selfish ambition. Keep affluent ones from becoming arrogant. Teach them to put their hope in You rather than wealth, as they are generous and rich in good deeds. Preserve their humility whenever they receive praise from others (James 3:16; 1 Timothy 6:17-18; Romans 12:3).

7. God of endurance and encouragement, give those called by Your Name in the media a spirit of unity among themselves as they follow Christ Jesus. Show them ways to encourage, support, and build each other up (Romans 15:5; 1 Thessalonians 5:11).

8. Holy Spirit, remind Christians in the media to be sober and watchful so they can resist and overcome the enemy who is seeking to devour them (Romans 8:37; 1 Peter 5:8-9).

9. Lord of love, cause the love of Christians to abound in knowledge and depth of insight so they can pray with discernment for those who have authority in the media industry. Raise up intercessors who will commit to put on their armor and tear down industry strongholds in the fight against the kingdom of darkness (Philippians 1:9-11; 1 Timothy 2:1-2; 2 Corinthians 10:3-4; Ephesians 6:12-13).

10. Lord of hosts, send legions of angels to the major media centers of the world such as Hollywood and New York to assist in spreading Your message and accomplishing Your will (Exodus 23:20; Acts 5:19-20).

11. Father, give wisdom, knowledge, and understanding to media leaders as they make decisions in program development. Save them from the ways and words of worldly wisdom. Keep them from receiving counsel from those who walk outside Your truth and who have cynical attitudes. Remove the influence of anything evil, perverse, and faithless (Proverbs 2:6, 12-15; 1 Corinthians 3:19; Psalms 1:1, 101:3-4).

12. O God, create in industry decision-makers a sensitivity to the power that words and images have for good or evil. Remind them that they will have to give an account for their decisions (Proverbs 18:21; Matthew 12:36).

13. Enable the media to see children as You see them,

Father, and to use caution and discernment in seeking to protect their innocence (Mark 9:42).

14. Creator God, You hold marriage and family relationships in high regard. Cause them to be portrayed in and through the media as good and honorable (Hebrews 13:4).

15. Lord, bring media themes and products that communicate Your truth into the forefront. Guide people to create entertainment that encourages positive life choices that are true, noble, right, pure, lovely, admirable, excellent, and praiseworthy (Deuteronomy 30:19; Philippians 4:8).

16. In the powerful name of Jesus, we stand against the power and influence of the occult in media and media products, as this leads to the downfall of a nation (Deuteronomy 18:10-12).

17. By Your grace, O God, teach Christian viewers to say "no" to ungodliness and worldly passions and to be self-controlled in their media choices. Teach them to lay hold of Your promises so they may escape corruption in the world. Holy Spirit, convict them of double-mindedness that sends mixed messages to program producers (Titus 2:11-12; 2 Peter 1:3-4; James 4:8).

18. Give Christian media ministries favor with You and with others. Remind them to seek Your kingdom first so all their physical needs will be supplied (Luke 2:52, 12:31).

19. God of Abraham, Isaac, and Israel, reveal Yourself as Savior and Redeemer through Christ the Messiah to Jewish media professionals. Cause them to turn to You so the veil that covers their hearts will be removed (Isaiah 60:16; 2 Corinthians 3:15-16).

20. Lord of the harvest, provide celebrities, media professionals, and their families with radical, life-changing encounters with You. Use them as chosen instruments to take your message to people in high places (Acts 9:1-19).

21. Father, with an expectant heart, I ask You to draw (name of someone in the media) to Yourself. Pierce (name's) heart with the good news about Your love. Lead (name) to repentance through Your kindness (John 6:44; Acts 2:37-38; Romans 2:4).

LARRY POLAND is the chairman and CEO of Mastermedia International, Inc., a ministry that reaches out with the gospel to leaders in Hollywood. For more information, go to www.mastermediaintl.org. This article is taken from *Pray!*, Issue 37, pp. 41-43. To order this article as a full-color bookmark prayer guide (50 per pack), call 1-800-366-7788 and ask for item #254, or go to www.praymag.com.

August

hearing his voice

"The ideal for hearing from God is finally determined by who God is, what kind of beings we are and what a personal relationship between ourselves and God should be like. Our failure to hear God has its deepest roots in a failure to understand, accept and grow into a conversational relationship with God, the sort of relationship suited to friends who are mature personalities in a shared enterprise, no matter how different they may be in other respects."

—Dallas Willard

Dallas Willard, *Hearing God* (Downers Grove, IL: InterVarsity Press, 1991, 1993, 1999), p. 29.

The LORD said, "Go out and stand on the mountain in the presence of the LORD, for the LORD is about to pass by." Then a great and powerful wind tore the mountains apart and shattered the rocks before the LORD, but the LORD was not in the wind. After the wind there was an earthquake, but the LORD was not in the earthquake. After the earthquake came a fire, but the LORD was not in the fire. And after the fire came a gentle whisper.

—1 Kings 19:11,12

August 1 · 1 Corinthians 12-14, Psalm 95

August 2 · 1 Corinthians 15-16, Psalm 96

August 3 · 2 Chronicles 1-4, Psalm 97

August 4 · 2 Chronicles 5-7, Psalm 98

_____

_____

_____

_____

_____

_____

_____

_____

_____

_____

August 5 · 2 Chronicles 8-11, Psalm 99

_____

_____

_____

_____

_____

_____

_____

_____

_____

_____

August 6 · 2 Chronicles 12-15, Psalm 100

_____

_____

_____

_____

_____

_____

_____

_____

_____

_____

still, small voice

How can we "hear" God? Can we hear His voice with our ears, just like we hear a call for dinner?

Usually, hearing God means that our hearts receive an idea from Him. Here's an example: I can point to the sky and say out loud, "The sky is blue." But I can also close my eyes and say silently in my mind, _The sky is blue._

To me, the words said in my mind are just as clear as those spoken out loud. They are real words, even though my ears can't hear them. When we hear like this from God, it is called the "still, small voice of God."

—Dick Eastman
(_Pray_Kids!, p. 1, _Pray!_,
Issue 29, p. 17.)

> **So Eli told Samuel, "Go and lie down,** and if he calls you, say, 'Speak, LORD, for your servant is listening.'" So Samuel went and lay down in his place. The LORD came and stood there, calling as at the other times, "Samuel! Samuel!" Then Samuel said, "Speak, for your servant is listening."
>
> —1 Samuel 3:9,10

AUGUST 7 · *Reflection*

AUGUST 8 · 2 Chronicles 16–18, Psalm 101

AUGUST 9 · 2 Chronicles 19–21, Psalm 102

A Listening Ear

If you're seeking to hear from God on a particular issue, find a quiet place where you can spend time in God's Word and then listen. Write down the thoughts that come to your mind.

AUGUST 10 · 2 Chronicles 22-24, Psalm 103

AUGUST 11 · 2 Chronicles 25-27, Psalm 104

AUGUST 12 · 2 Chronicles 28-30, Psalm 105

If you feel God is giving you a specific plan of action, check to see if you can find confirmation in Scripture. Then ask God to confirm His Word to you through godly people. Those in leadership especially need to find people who are not afraid to disagree with them. There may be times, however, when God tells you to do something and godly counsel disagrees. Those times—if they ever happen—will be rare. If such a time does occur, look for a peace in your spirit as proof that you should still move ahead.

If you get the go-ahead from Scripture and godly counsel, then it is safe to consider circumstances. A common mistake is to look first at circumstances and then reason, "Look how everything just fell into place. This must be God." We always need the confirmation of Scripture and of godly counsel.

—Marilyn Willett Heavilin
(*Pray!*, Issue 13, p. 20.)

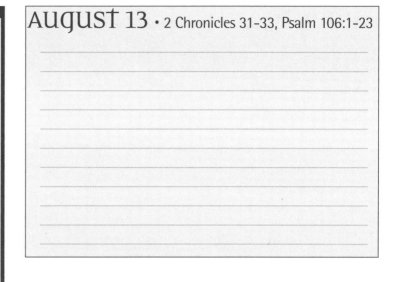

Guard your steps when you go to the house of God. Go near to listen rather than to offer the sacrifice of fools, who do not know that they do wrong. Do not be quick with your mouth, do not be hasty in your heart to utter anything before God. God is in heaven and you are on earth, so let your words be few.

—Ecclesiastes 5:1,2

AUGUST 13 · 2 Chronicles 31–33, Psalm 106:1-23

AUGUST 14 · *Reflection*

AUGUST 15 · 2 Chronicles 34–36, Psalm 106:24-48

"I know the Feeling"

Some 25 years ago, when I was a new believer, I learned both about the importance of giving God praise as well as letting my

AUGUST 16 · Obediah, Psalm 107

AUGUST 17 · 2 Corinthians 1-3, Psalm 108

AUGUST 18 · 2 Corinthians 4-6, Psalm 109

words be few. God spoke to me. While it was not in an audible voice, I knew beyond a shadow of a doubt that it was Him.

It was at a marriage retreat that my wife, Cindy, and I were attending. I was standing behind her, trying to gently ease some of the tension out of her neck. As this was taking place, the pastor began to speak about the need for couples to encourage one another. While I didn't deserve much encouragement in those days, that didn't stop me from asking God to convict Cindy's heart. "She never praises me!"

As soon as I finished that brief prayer, I heard God say, "I know the feeling." Ouch! He continued, "Get your eyes off of Cindy and begin to praise Me." Wow!

—Vince D'Acchioli
On Target Ministries,
www.otm.org.

> **Now when he saw** the crowds, he went up on a mountainside and sat down. His disciples came to him, and he began to teach them.
>
> —Matthew 5:1,2

August 19 · 2 Corinthians 7-9, Psalm 110

August 20 · 2 Corinthians 10-13, Psalm 111

in the outdoors

When Jesus really wanted His disciples' undivided attention, He took them to the mountain as well as to many other places away from the rush of "suburban" Jerusalem life.

Picture the smoke rising from a crackling campfire on Galilee

August 21 · *Reflection*

August 22 · Ezra 1-4, Psalm 112

August 23 · Ezra 5-7, Psalm 113

August 24 · Ezra 8-10, Psalm 114

Beach. The stars are sparkling overhead. Thirteen close friends, having rowed across the white-caps earlier in the evening, are savoring a fish dinner and soaking up the warmth from the flickering orange flames. The conversations are light and sprinkled with laughter.

In a momentary lull, the Master looks up with a smile and says, "I want to tell you something very important." All eyes are on Him as He continues.

The Master still speaks today. He wants to tell you something very important. Take time out and come hear what He has to say. He doesn't speak any louder in the outdoors; it's just easier to hear Him.

—John Ashmen
Christian Camping
International

> "For I know the plans I have for you," declares the LORD, "plans to prosper you and not to harm you, plans to give you hope and a future."
>
> —Jeremiah 29:11

AUGUST 25 · Nehemiah 1–3, Psalm 115

AUGUST 26 · Nehemiah 4–7, Psalm 116

AUGUST 27 · Nehemiah 8–10, Psalm 117

God still speaks

"I'm sorry, your baby is born with a birth defect." These words from the delivery doctor turned my world upside down. Instead of rejoicing over the birth of our second child, grief and sadness filled our world.

August 28 · Nehemiah 11–13, Psalm 118

The thought that Daniel would never be a "normal" child crushed me.

Six months later, while still trying to sort things out, God convicted me about fasting for my son. I had fasted several times before, but never for something so personal. That morning, I began a 30-day fast—my longest ever.

August 29 · *Reflection*

During my fast, God spoke to my heart. He told me that one day Daniel would walk and talk. He gave me Jeremiah 29:11 as a confirmation. He drew me close and healed my hurts. Today, Daniel is an active, walking, and talking young man who loves Jesus. And his dad does, too!

—Allen Tilley
(*Pray!*, Issue 3, p. 28.)

August 30 · *Reflection*

August 31 · *Reflection*

monthly reflection

What is the Spirit of God saying to me this month? What is my response?

prayer for the month:

Lord, when I consider how well I listen, I know I need You to teach me how to do it better. Let me be like Mary who chose sitting at Your feet, listening to what You had to say. Help me pay attention and not be distracted. Give me ears to hear what Your Spirit is saying and a heart that stays tender in response. Guide me with Your voice as I walk through my day (Luke 8:18, 10:38-42; Revelation 3:22; Hebrews 4:7; Isaiah 30:21).

18 Prayers for Higher Education

By Mistie Hutchison

We all know people who became radically devoted to Jesus during their college years and went on to influence society in significant ways. Sadly, most of us also know some who rebelled during those impressionable years. You can help college and university students at this pivotal time in their lives by using these prayers to direct you into strategic intercession.

Evangelism

1. God, open the door for the message of Christ to be proclaimed on university and college campuses. Give Your people words and boldness to make it known. Open the hearts of students, faculty, and administrators so they can respond to the message. Once they do, Lord, please let the message spread rapidly (Colossians 4:3-4; Ephesians 6:19; Acts 16:14; 2 Thessalonians 3:1).

Students

2. Lord, give students a hunger for truth and a curiosity about Your Word, followed by an understanding and love for it (Psalm 119:97,104).

3. Faithful God, help Christian students to become "longhaulers" who will stand firm and follow You for their entire lives and not just during their college days. Let nothing move them away from You. Give them grace to always devote themselves fully to Your work because they know their labor for You is not in vain (1 Corinthians 15:58).

4. Holy Spirit, convict believing students of sin and help them to abstain from it wholeheartedly. Empower them to live such good lives that their unbelieving peers will see their good deeds and give You glory (1 Peter 2:11-12).

Faculty and Administration

5. God of all wisdom, help these learned men and women not to be puffed up by their knowledge. Give them humility so they will not be caught in the trap of thinking they know it all. Help them to recognize that the foolishness of God is wiser than all of human wisdom (1 Corinthians 1:20-25, 8:1-2).

6. Spirit of truth, guide professors and textbook writers into all truth. Demolish strongholds of worldly godless philosophies; demolish every argument and pretension that sets itself up against the knowledge of God. Help curriculum creators focus on what is true, noble, right, pure, lovely, admirable, excellent, and praiseworthy (John 16:13; 2 Corinthians 10:4-5; Philippians 4:8).

7. Lord, raise up a generation of godly faculty and administrators—young people with aptitude for every kind of learning, who are well informed, quick to understand, and able to teach even in a godless environment (Daniel 1:4).

Gender

8. Creator God, give young adults delight in their masculinity and femininity, and the fact that You made both genders in Your image. Help them to glorify and thank You so their thinking doesn't become futile, their hearts darkened, and their sexuality confused (Genesis 1:27; Romans 1:21,24,26-27).

Student Leaders

9. Sovereign Lord, You establish all authorities, including campus housing administrators and residence hall directors. Bring students who hold authority positions to the knowledge of the truth so that everyone may live peaceful and quiet lives in all godliness and holiness (Romans 13:1; 1 Timothy 2:1-3).

10. Light of the world, shine into the influential Greek system. Remove the veil from those whom the god of this age has blinded so they can see the gospel of Christ, who is the image of God. Help those who have pledged fraternities and sororities to follow Your great light so they will never walk in darkness, but will have the light of life (John 1:5; 2 Corinthians 4:3-4; John 8:12).

11. Bless Christian athletes as they run the race You have for them. Help them to pursue not only earthly trophies, but also the eternal prize. May they hold out the word of life so

they may boast on the day of Christ that they did not run for nothing (Hebrews 12:1; 1 Corinthians 9:24-25; Philippians 2:16).

campus ministries

12. Lord, cause campus ministries to delight in revering Your name. Grant them favor with college administrators and faculty (Nehemiah 1:11).

13. Jehovah-Jireh, provide for all the campus ministers' needs according to Your glorious riches in Christ Jesus. Raise up supportive believers who will plead for the privilege of sharing in this service (Philippians 4:19; 2 Corinthians 8:4).

14. Lord of the harvest, send workers into the academic harvest field, especially where Christ is not yet known and where they will not have to build on someone else's foundation (Matthew 9:38; John 4:35; Romans 15:20).

spiritual warfare

15. Father, shield students from the hollow and deceptive philosophies, human traditions, and worldly principles on college campuses (Colossians 2:8).

16. Deliverer, protect believing students and faculty from evildoers and enemies. Strengthen and protect them from the evil one, and direct their hearts into Your love and Christ's perseverance (Psalm 59:1-2; 2 Thessalonians 3:3,5).

missions

17. Lord of the nations, You determined the times and exact places where all people live so they would seek You. Inspire international students to find You while they are abroad. When they return home, cause them to tell their own people what You have done for them (Acts 17:26-27; Luke 8:39).

18. Father, You have prepared good works for all Your children. Raise up new Christian leaders and send them into government, business, education, journalism, and the arts so they can make disciples of all nations (Ephesians 2:10; Matthew 28:19).

MISTIE HUTCHISON works for EDGE Corps, a division of The Navigators that ministers to college students. This article is adapted from *Pray!*, Issue 39, pp. 52-55. To order this article as a full color, bookmark prayer guide (50 per pack), call 1-800-366-7788, and ask for item #238, or go to www.praymag.com.

september

trusting His way

"We should pray for deliverance, and we should learn to resist the attacks of Satan in the power of Jesus Christ. But we should always pray in an attitude of humble acceptance of that which is God's will. Sometimes God's will is deliverance from the adversity; sometimes it is the provision of grace to accept the adversity. Trusting God for the grace to accept adversity is as much an act of faith as is trusting Him for deliverance from it."

—Jerry Bridges

Jerry Bridges, *Trusting God* (Colorado Springs, CO: NavPress, 1988), p. 213.

> **Your attitude should be the same** as that of Christ Jesus: Who, being in very nature God, did not consider equality with God something to be grasped, but made himself nothing, taking the very nature of a servant, being made in human likeness. And being found in appearance as a man, he humbled himself and became obedient to death—even death on a cross!
>
> —Philippians 2:5-8

one way

Jesus began (Luke 3:21) and ended (Luke 23:46) His ministry on earth with prayer. In between there are more than 45 Scripture references to Jesus praying. But

september 1 · 1 Timothy 1-3,
Psalm 119:1-8

september 2 · 1 Timothy 4-6,
Psalm 119:9-16

september 3 · Esther 1-3,
Psalm 119:17-24

september 4 • Esther 4-7,
Psalm 119:25-32

september 5 • Esther 8-10,
Psalm 119:33-40

september 6 • 2 Timothy,
Psalm 119:41-48

His focus didn't seem to be on the *act* of praying as much as on prayerful *dependence* upon His Father. In so doing, Jesus modeled seeking the Father's will and trusting the Father's way.

Throughout His life, Jesus stated that:

• What He taught was not His own (John 7:16)

• He could do nothing by Himself (John 5:19, 8:28)

• He did what He saw His Father doing (John 5:19-20, 8:38)

• He taught what His Father taught Him (John 8:28)

• What He heard and learned from His Father He taught to His disciples (John 15:15, 17:7)

• The Father who sent Him commanded Him what to say and how to say it (John 12:49)

These are all examples of a will perfectly molded through powerful and constant prayer. Could we make these same statements?

—Dann Spader

(*Pray!*, Issue 14, pp. 16-17.)

> "Father, if you are willing, take this cup from me; yet not my will, but yours be done."
>
> —Luke 22:42

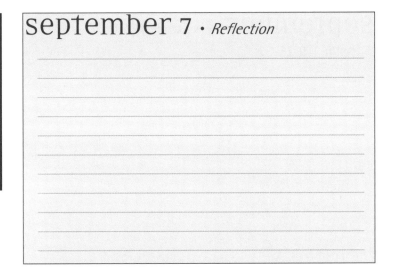

september 7 · *Reflection*

september 8 · Job 1–3, Psalm 119:49–56

Fully conformed

As you relinquish the very thing you crave, you are expressing the willingness to conform to His will. Take Jesus in Gethsemane as an example. Facing the cross, He prayed that if it be the Father's will that the cup would be taken from Him—"yet not my will, but yours be done."

september 9 · Job 4–6, Psalm 119:57–64

september 10 · Job 7-9, Psalm 119:65-72

september 11 · Job 10-12, Psalm 119:73-80

september 12 · Job 13-15, Psalm 119:81-88

What Jesus was asking was obviously not sinful. He was not rebelling against God's will. He was saying, "If there's any other way to accomplish your purposes and bring glory to Your name . . . " He asked for God's will to change, but He was committed to conforming to it nevertheless.

Conforming to God's will is not merely surrender. Neither is it a fatalistic declaration that everything that happens is God's will. Jesus' own desire remained intense. But He still said, "Though I deeply want to be spared the cross, I prefer Your will to My own."

—Janet Leighton
(*Pray!*, Issue 35, p. 37.)

> **Delight yourself in the LORD** and he will give you the desires of your heart. Commit your way to the LORD; trust in him and he will do this.
>
> —Psalm 37:4,5

september 13 · Job 16-18, Psalm 119:89-96

september 14 · *Reflection*

GOD MY GUIDE

We must submit to where our Lord leads and what He commands, even if He sends us in a direction we don't want to go.

It's a bit like river rafting with an experienced guide. You may

september 15 · Job 19-21, Psalm 119:97-104

september 16 · Job 22-24,
Psalm 119:105-112

september 17 · Job 25-27,
Psalm 119:113-120

september 18 · Job 28-30,
Psalm 119:121-128

begin to panic when the guide steers you straight into a steep waterfall, especially if another course appears much safer. Yet after you've emerged from the swirling depths and wiped the spray from your eyes, you see that just beyond the seemingly "safe" route was a series of jagged rocks. Your guide knew what he was doing after all.

When we yield to the Lord's leading, we discover the additional truth that followed Jesus' statements that we who are weary and burdened can come to Him and find rest, take His yoke upon us and learn from Him. He added, "I am gentle and humble in heart, and you will find rest for your souls. For my yoke is easy and my burden is light" (see Matthew 11:28-30).

—Shirley Dobson
(*Pray!*, Issue 31, p. 38.)

> **"Which of you, if his son asks for bread,** will give him a stone? Or if he asks for a fish, will give him a snake? If you, then, though you are evil, know how to give good gifts to your children, how much more will your Father in heaven give good gifts to those who ask him!"
>
> —Matthew 7:9-11

september 19 · Job 31-33,
Psalm 119:129-136

september 20 · Job 34-36,
Psalm 119:137-144

september 21 · *Reflection*

FaTHer Knows BesT

Daniel, our first son, was born with a congenital heart problem. One of the problems with

september 22 · Job 37-39,
Psalm 119:145-152

_____
_____
_____
_____
_____
_____
_____
_____
_____

september 23 · Job 40-42,
Psalm 119:153-160

_____
_____
_____
_____
_____
_____
_____
_____
_____

september 24 · Titus, Psalm 119:161-168

_____
_____
_____
_____
_____
_____
_____
_____
_____
_____

his little heart was multiple septal defects; he had several openings between the two chambers of the heart. We prayed that God would heal those holes.

Several months and more tests later, we learned the full nature of his heart problem—the reverse position of the main arteries leading to the heart. If the septal defects had closed, Daniel would have died immediately because his heart couldn't have functioned at all.

Our great and good Heavenly Father sometimes doesn't answer our petitions because He knows so much better than we do what is best. This confidence in God's goodness carried us through when Daniel eventually died at age two.

—Dennis Cone

> "Now, Lord, con-
> sider their threats and
> enable your servants to
> speak your word with great
> boldness. Stretch out your
> hand to heal and perform
> miraculous signs and won-
> ders through the name of
> your holy servant Jesus."
>
> -Acts 4:29,30

september 25 • Jeremiah 1-3, Psalm 119:169-176

september 26 • Jeremiah 4-6, Psalm 120

september 27 • Jeremiah 7-9, Psalm 121

In Times of crisis

When we face a crisis, how will
we pray? In Acts 4:24-30, this
group of believers asked themselves, "What do we need in
order to best colabor with God
in His sovereign work on

september 28 · Jeremiah 10-12, Psalm 122

september 29 · *Reflection*

september 30 · *Reflection*

earth?" The answer to that question became a prayer request (see vv. 29-30).

God may not lead us to ask the same specific requests these early disciples asked. However, we do need to learn from them how to see our situation from God's perspective. Asking is the easy part of praying. Knowing what to ask takes time and reasoning with God through the Scriptures.

A good starting place would be to ask God the question, "Amid this crisis, what do I need in order to best colabor with You, Lord, in Your sovereign work on earth?" Seek to join God in His purposes. Look to Him as opposed to looking for the easy way out.

—Lee Brase
(*Pray!*, Issue 1, p. 30.)

notes

_____

_____

_____

_____

_____

_____

_____

_____

_____

_____

_____

_____

monthly reflection

What is the Spirit of God saying to me this month? What is my response?

_____

_____

_____

_____

_____

_____

_____

_____

_____

_____

prayer for the month:

Your ways aren't my ways, Father, but they are perfect. Show me Your ways and teach me Your paths—I will trust You with all my heart even when I don't understand. Your love is unfailing—let me sense that each morning as I put my trust in You. Help me stay committed to Your way as I trust because there's no God for me but You (Isaiah 55:8; Psalm 18:30, 25:4; Proverbs 3:5; Psalms 143:8, 37:5, 31:14).

Power-Packed Prayers for Public Schools

By Ida Rose Heckard

Metal detectors won't do it. Gun control won't either. Nor will carefully crafted self-esteem programs. Nothing humans dream up will cure what ails America's public schools. But prayer can.

Each time school violence erupts, I see faces of kids I've worked with as a public school psychologist who could just as easily pull the trigger. Kids like "Jason," an awkward, freckle-faced, 14-year-old boy with fetal alcohol syndrome. Jason's mom still drinks heavily, attempting to dull the pain of severe domestic violence. When his parents fight, he stays away for days. Jason is a ticking bomb.

But violence is only the smoking crater atop a smoldering volcano. Contentious issues churn in every school. While working for the public schools, I met each week with a prayer partner and prayed fervently for the spiritual needs of the schools I covered. Over time, many "Jasons" turned around. God called a committed Christian principal to fill a vacated position. Corruption in administration and conflict among staff were exposed and healed.

You can turn things around in public schools, too. Here's a list of 31 prayers that target the heat of the battle in your neighborhood school.

1. Love. "Father, may the students and staff of this school experience Your love through the Christians they know in profound and authentic ways" (John 13:35).

2. Repentance of Christians. "May the students and staff of this school who have been hurt by the careless or unkind words or deeds of Christians find healing and forgiveness through the repentance of Christians they know" (1 Corinthians 10:32).

3. Peace. "May the peace that surpasses all understanding rule the hearts and minds of every student, teacher, administrator, and staff member in this school" (Philippians 4:7).

4. Truth. "Lord, release truth in this school. Help students to rightly discern truth and not believe false teachings" (Proverbs 23:23).

5. Integrity. "I pray that any financial, educational, administrative, or sexual corruption that affects this school would be exposed and healed" (Proverbs 11:3).

6. School board. "I pray blessings on each school board member (try to pray for them by name). Father, may Your will be done at board meetings" (Romans 13:1).

7. Principal. "May [name of principal] recognize the God-given responsibility he/she has for the best interests of the children who attend the school. May [name of principal] walk in wisdom, integrity, grace, and truth" (Proverbs 2:1-11).

8. Teachers who are not yet believers. "Bring all the teachers in this school who do not yet know You into Your kingdom. Arrange divine appointments, that they may have a profound encounter with Your Word" (Romans 5:8).

9. Christian teachers. "Grant wisdom, Lord, for the Christian teachers in this school as they seek to live out their faith. Help them be salt and light. Protect them from doubt and fear. Strengthen their faith by drawing them into Your Word, prayer, and fellowship with other believers" (Hebrews 10:25).

10. Support staff. "Father, may the social workers, psychologists, speech therapists, nurses, custodians, aides, and other professional support staff treat students with dignity and respect. May all their interventions be based on truth and not on human theories" (1 Corinthians 1:19-21).

11. Special education decisions. "Lord, may those involved in making decisions for children with special learning and emotional needs make those decisions based on what is best for the child and according to what is right" (Isaiah 56:1).

12. Parents. "Father, guide the parents of the students at this school as they parent. Give them the courage to lovingly discipline their children. Turn the hearts of the fathers and mothers toward their children" (Deuteronomy 6:7; Malachi 4:6; Ephesians 6:4).

13. Rejected students. "Lord, come alongside those children who feel rejected by their peers or teachers. Plant people in their lives who will love them unconditionally. In your divine wisdom, Lord, convict the students and teachers who ostracize these children" (Isaiah 1:17).

14. Failing students. "Lord, I ask You to encourage those children who are struggling with their studies. Strengthen their minds. Help their teachers and parents know how to help them learn. Protect them from feelings of worthlessness and shame" (1 Thessalonians 5:14).

15. Children of divorce, abuse, and neglect. "Father of the fatherless, heal the children of this school whose homes and hearts are ravaged by divorce, abandonment, or domestic violence. Protect them from physical harm and emotional scars. Bring people to them who will pour Your healing Word into the broken places of their hearts" (James 1:27).

16. Children with emotional disturbance. "God, work Your healing grace in the life of every emotionally disturbed child who attends this school. Protect them and others from the anger, hurt, and fear that ensnares them" (Matthew 15:22-28).

17. Violence. "Lord, stay the hand of violence against the children and staff of this school. Dismantle any plan to bring harm to them. Expose any weapon brought onto the school premises and render it harmless" (Psalm 34:7, 57:1).

18. Suicide. "God, stand against any suicidal thoughts, actions, and plans that would tempt the students or staff of this school to take their own lives. Comfort and speak truth to those who are in such despair that life doesn't seem worth living" (Isaiah 66:13; 2 Corinthians 1:3).

19. Forces of evil. "In the name of Jesus, I pray that all spiritual forces that would deceive the minds of the children and staff of this school into practicing any form of witchcraft or divination would be rendered powerless" (Isaiah 8:19-20; Micah 5:12).

20. Evolution. "Father God, may the children of this school come to know You as their Creator. May the teachers and curriculum tell them the truth about the origin of the universe" (Genesis 1:1; Psalm 14:1).

21. Sexual purity. "May the students of this school grow up honoring their sexuality and committing themselves to sexual abstinence until marriage. Give them the grace they need to live out this commitment" (1 Thessalonians 4:3-5).

22. Drugs and alcohol. "Release any students or staff members of this school from the addictive power of illegal drugs and alcohol. Expose and convict those who sell illegal substances to the children of this school" (Psalm 37:32-33).

23. Christian programs. "Father, I pray for abundant blessings on programs that bring Christ into this public school. Help the groups who sponsor such programs function according to Your Word and in harmony with each other. Bless the leaders and bring forth new and growing believers" (1 Corinthians 12:12-13).

24. Christian students. "Grant the Christian students who attend this school wisdom and boldness in living out their faith. Help them share effectively the good news of salvation through Jesus Christ with their classmates" (1 Timothy 4:12).

25. A chosen generation. "Father, may your kingdom come. From the students at this school, raise up a generation of people who worship You in spirit and in truth" (John 4:23-24; 1 Peter 2:9).

26. An open door. "Lord, may there be an open door in this school for the gospel to be shared with students and staff. Allow full advantage to be taken of every opportunity to name the name of Jesus" (Matthew 7:7; 1 Corinthians 16:9).

IDA ROSE HECKARD is an education specialist, a free-lance writer, and a pastor's wife from Kahului, Hawaii. This article is taken from *Pray!*, Issue 20, pp. 26-29. To order this article as a full-color bookmark prayer guide (50 per pack), call 1-800-366-7788, and ask for item #1052, or go to www.praymag.com.

october

obeying His word

"Obey God in the thing He shows you, and instantly the next thing is opened up. One reads tomes on the work of the Holy Spirit, when one five minutes of drastic obedience would make things as clear as a sunbeam. 'I suppose I shall understand these things some day!' You can understand them now. It is not study that does it, but obedience. The tiniest fragment of obedience, and heaven opens and the profoundest truths of God are yours straight away. God will never reveal more truth about Himself until you have obeyed what you know already."

—Oswald Chambers

Oswald Chambers, *My Utmost for His Highest* (Westwood, NJ: Barbour and Company, Inc., 1935, 1963), p. 210.

> **"The watchman opens the gate for him,** and the sheep listen to his voice. He calls his own sheep by name and leads them out. . . . My sheep listen to my voice; I know them, and they follow me."
>
> —John 10:3,27

one yes at a time

"Take care of small obediences," I sensed the Lord tell me as I prayed. "If you want to live out what I want to do in your life in the 'big' things, you must do what I say, when I say it, the way I say to do it, in the 'small' things."

october 1 · Jeremiah 13-15, Isaiah 1-2

october 2 · Jeremiah 16-18, Isaiah 3

october 3 · Jeremiah 19-21, Isaiah 4-5

october 4 · Jeremiah 22-24, Isaiah 6

october 5 · Jeremiah 25-27, Isaiah 7-8

october 6 · Jeremiah 28-30, Isaiah 9

"I want whatever You want, Your will in my life, moment by moment," I replied. "I know that lifestyle obedience needs to be lived one 'yes, Lord' at a time. It is the place of close communication with You, sensitive to Your gentlest whisper."

"You will know My voice by talking constantly with Me, by being daily in My Word, by letting My Holy Spirit fill you. Wait before Me to hear My agenda for your day. Relinquish your ideas and plans to Me. See Me in the smallest details."

This is my prayer, for myself and the body of Christ. May we, His sheep, hear and obey His voice.

—Sylvia Gunter
(*Pray!*, Issue 26, p. 32.)

> "I tell you the truth, the Son can do nothing by himself; he can only do what he sees the Father doing, because whatever the Father does the Son also does."
>
> —John 5:19

october 7 · *Reflection*

october 8 · Jeremiah 31-33, Isaiah 10-11

october 9 · Jeremiah 34-36, Isaiah 12

nudged by the spirit

Recently, I spoke to a friend about spiritual warfare. I explained that for years Christians had encouraged me to learn about it, but I was never comfortable in that arena. My motto was, "If I leave Satan alone, he'll leave me alone."

october 10 • Jeremiah 37-39, Isaiah 13-14

During the conversation, she alluded to the fact that understanding spiritual warfare would change my prayer life. Immediately, the Holy Spirit moved on my heart, and I knew it was time for me to step into this uncharted territory.

The Spirit of God pointed out my disobedience. So I began to read Christian resources on spiritual warfare, such as C. S. Lewis' *The Screwtape Letters*, among others. What I learned in the process completely changed my prayer life, my attitude toward prayer, and my understanding of prayer's relationship to angels and demons.

—Vanita Warren

(*Pray!*, Issue 30, pp. 50-51.)

october 11 • Jeremiah 40-42, Isaiah 15

october 12 • Jeremiah 43-46, Isaiah 16-17

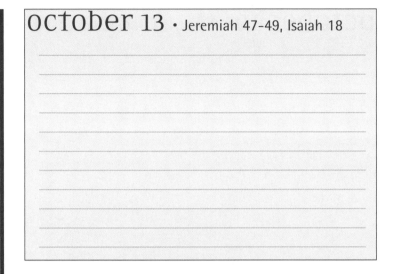

october 13 · Jeremiah 47-49, Isaiah 18

october 14 · *Reflection*

october 15 · Jeremiah 50-52, Isaiah 19-20

words to live by

How can you know whether a biblical promise is God's word for you, one that He wants you to claim as His word to you? When you approach a particular biblical promise, attempt to understand the original historical

october 16 · 1 John 1-3, Isaiah 21

october 17 · 1 John 4-5, Isaiah 22-23

october 18 · Lamentations 1-3, Isaiah 24

context, look carefully at your current circumstances to see if it's a parallel situation, and look at the broader biblical context to see if there's anything that should cause you to be cautious in claiming the promise. Then pray over it and ask God if He wants you to claim it.

As you pray, if you sense freedom in your spirit to claim it, there is a high probability that God is speaking it to you personally. If there is reluctance in your spirit, then don't consider the promise for yourself until God gives you more light and understanding.

Finally, share the promise with trusted believers. If they affirm it, then claim it and move out on it. If they fail to affirm it, exercise utmost caution.

—Alan Andrews
(*Pray!*, Issue 24, pp. 22-23.)

october 19 · Lamentations 4–5, Isaiah 25–26

october 20 · 2 & 3 John, Isaiah 27

october 21 · *Reflection*

obey Anyway

"Where are we going?" my children asked as I turned the car around. What reasonable explanation could I give them? *Go, get gas*, the thought crossed my mind. All I could say was, "I have a strange feeling . . . that . . . we're supposed to get gas."

october 22 · 1 Peter 1-3, Isaiah 28-29

october 23 · 1 Peter 4-5, Isaiah 30

october 24 · Ezekiel 1-4, Isaiah 31-32

Okay, Lord, I prayed as I finished pumping a few drops into my tank. *I'm here; I don't know why, but I'm here.* I paid, and as I was heading back to the car a woman with dark sunglasses reached for my arm. "You've got to pray for me," she blurted.

From behind her sunglasses, tears trickled down her cheeks. "I've seen you at church, and I really need you to pray for me." I committed to do so, gave her a hug, and she climbed into the driver's seat of her car and looked back at me. "I prayed for God to send me someone to talk to—you were His answer."

—Kathleen Swartz McQuaig
(*Pray!*, Issue 13, p. 12.)

> "Has not my hand made all these things, and so they came into being?" declares the LORD. "This is the one I esteem: he who is humble and contrite in spirit, and trembles at my word."
>
> —Isaiah 66:2

october 25 · Ezekiel 5-7, Isaiah 33

october 26 · Ezekiel 8-11, Isaiah 34-35

october 27 · Ezekiel 12-16, Isaiah 36-37

surprised by joy

My youngest brother, Eric, was a mess during his late teens and twenties. One beer and his eyes glazed over; add drugs and that's a destructive mix. There was a time Eric lived on the street, because no one in the family could trust him.

october 28 · Ezekiel 17-19, Isaiah 38-39

october 29 · *Reflection*

october 30 · *Reflection*

Eric experienced an Apostle Paul-like conversion one day when he "happened" into a church with "Victory" in its name. So transformed was he that he began to talk in "King James" and take God's Word seriously.

During these days Mom called me and said, "Did you hear the latest with Eric?" I braced for the worst—could he have backslidden? "He gave away his car!" It was the only thing of value to his name, and barely streetworthy! He'd learned of a single mother's need for transportation, remembered what God says about having pity on the needy (1 John 3:17), and heard God tell him to give her his car. He did so with joy!

Speaking of Joy, that's my mom's name. Eric called Mom—always a "religious" woman but apart from Christ—to ask a favor: "Can you give me a ride to church today?" We praise God that she did, because that's the day she heard the gospel and prayed "the sinner's prayer," which she signed and glued in the front of her Bible!

—Dean Ridings

october 31 · *Reflection*

---

monthly reflection

What is the Spirit of God saying to me this month? What is my response?

---

prayer for the month:

Lord, You have said that to obey is better than sacrifice. You delight in our obedience. Give me understanding so that I will obey Your Word with all my heart. Help me remember what I've received and heard from You. I'm responding to Your wake-up call so that I maintain an obedient and repentant heart. Help me work wholeheartedly at obedience to Your commands so that I display and walk in love (1 Samuel 15:22; Psalm 119:34; Revelation 3:2,3; 2 Chronicles 31:21; 2 John 1:6).

24 scripture-based prayers to pray for your pastor

By Terry Teykl

Pastors are under attack today as never before. That is why it is so important to hold them up in prayer. But unless they have requests or are aware of specific needs their pastors have, many people do not know what to pray on a regular basis for them.

Here are some sample Scripture-based prayers. Each one was written with a specific need in mind. You can use them one at a time, or pray all of them in the order you feel is best for the spiritual needs of your pastor.

These prayers are simply models and suggestions. Use them to get started or to get ideas about what to pray.

1. I thank You, Father, that Your eyes are on my shepherd and Your ears are attentive to my pastor's prayers and Your face is against those who plot evil against my pastor (1 Peter 3:12). For I know that in all things You work for the good of _____ (insert your pastor's name) who loves You (Romans 8:28). Who can accuse this pastor who is daily interceded for by Christ Jesus? (Romans 8:33-34). Therefore, in all things my pastor is more than a conqueror (Romans 8:37). Thank You, God.

2. Lord, I pray for discernment in exposing any schemes of the enemy against my pastor. Show our congregation how to pray against all powers of this dark world and the spiritual forces of darkness in heavenly realms. And, Lord, protect us as we wage warfare on behalf of our pastor (Ephesians 6:11-12).

3. Father, I thank You that no weapons formed against my pastor will prosper. Every tongue raised against my shepherd will be cast down. Rumors and gossip will be turned aside. For _____ will be still before the Lord and wait on You. My pastor will dwell in the shadow of the Most High God and will be delivered from terror, darts of doubt, and diseases (Psalm 91:5-6). Set Your angels about my pastor (Psalm 91:11) and no power of the enemy shall harm _____ (Luke 10:19). Thank God forevermore!

4. Lord, let _____ have a discerning mind to prioritize the precious minutes in the day. Let my pastor discern what is most important and be guarded against the tyranny of the urgent (2 Corinthians 11:14; 1 John 4:1).

5. Father, allow my pastor to glory only in the cross (Galatians 6:14). Keep my pastor from pride and pity. Let the cross be his reason for ministry.

6. Jesus keep my pastor holy in every way (1 Peter 1:16). Protect my shepherd from seducing spirits especially when he/she is tired and hard-pressed. Give _____ comrades to help protect him/her, and to share with in personal holiness (James 4:7). As my pastor draws near to You, draw near to my pastor (James 4:8).

7. I pray that the eyes of my pastor may be enlightened to know the hope to which we are called and know the riches of our glorious inheritance in the saints. Let my pastor know the incomparable great power which is in us who believe (Ephesians 1:18-19). Let _____ see the full revelation of Jesus Christ (Galatians 1:12). Place in him/her a desire to know Christ and the power of His resurrection (Philippians 3:10).

8. Lord, as my shepherd spends quiet time with You, shed Your love abroad in his/her heart. Let my pastor know how much he/she is loved (Romans 5:5). In Jesus' name let the love of God be my pastor's mainstay in ministry. So be it!

9. Lord, I lift up the hands of my pastor and his/her family. Place them in the shelter of the Most High to rest in the shadow of the Almighty. I will say of the Lord, You are their refuge and fortress. You will preserve their family time. You will cover their home. Your faithfulness will meet their financial needs in Christ Jesus (Philippians 4:19). You will command Your angels to guard them as they travel and win the lost. You have said, "I will be with [them] in trouble, I will deliver [them] and honor [them]. With a long life, will I satisfy [them] and show [them] my salvation" (Psalm 91:15-16). In Jesus' name I cancel all assignments of the enemy against them.

10. In Jesus' name I speak to church hurts, abuse, and ungrateful forces to move. I speak to mountains of criticism

and inordinate expectations to be cast into the sea. I speak to stress, excessive phone counseling, and fatigue to be cast into the sea, and I believe every need, vision, and dream of _____'s will be completed (Mark 11:22-24; Philippians 4:19).

11. Forgive those who hurt _____ and speak against him/her, and may my pastor walk in forgiveness (Ephesians 4:32-5:1). Guard my pastor from futile thinking (Ephesians 4:17) and a vain imagination. Let every thought be taken captive to obey Christ (2 Corinthians 10:3-5).

12. In Jesus' name I bind the fear of failure and the fear of humankind (John 14:1). Let _____'s confidence not be eroded by the daily resistance to the gospel or his/her vision. Allow my pastor to fear God more than people.

13. Father, heal my shepherd's heart of any grief caused by ministry. Bestow on my pastor a crown of beauty instead of ashes and anoint him/her with the oil of gladness instead of mourning. Clothe my shepherd with a garment of praise instead of a spirit of depression. I call my pastor an oak of righteousness, a planting of the Lord to display Your splendor (Isaiah 61:3).

14. Jesus, You said, "Do not let your hearts be troubled. Trust in God; trust also in me.... Peace I leave with you; my peace I give you" (John 14:1,27). Apply these promises to _____. Let my pastor know the plans You have for him/her, plans to prosper, plans to give hope and a future (Jeremiah 29:11).

15. Keep my pastor in the midst of good and exciting worship. Keep my pastor from the traditions of men and religion which hold the form of godliness, but deny its power (2 Timothy 3:5). Give _____ a vision of heaven (Isaiah 6; Revelation 4).

16. With my shield of faith I cover my shepherd's mind to quench all flaming darts of doubt or vain imagination or mental distractions (Ephesians 6:16; Colossians 2:6-8). Let the mind of Christ be strong in my pastor (1 Corinthians 2:16).

17. Lord, I stand against the enemies of my pastor's prayer life: "busyness" (Acts 6:2-4), compulsions, compromise (Acts 5), unnecessary phone calls, chronic counselees, fatigue, sleepiness (Matthew 26:41), appetites, television, late meetings, over-commitments, and doubt. Let nothing hinder _____'s time with You. Let my pastor rise up to seek You (Mark 1:35), pray with other pastors (Acts 1:14), and pray without ceasing (1 Thessalonians 5:17). Give my pas-

tor the time, the desire, and the place to pray (Acts 16:16). I rebuke in the name of Jesus any distractions from my pastor's devotional life.

18. Send the spirit of prayer upon _____ (Acts 1:8, Romans 8:26). Send others to join us in praying for our pastor (1 Timothy 2:1-8).

19. Bless my pastor with rich study time (Acts 6:4; 2 Timothy 2:15).

20. As _____ preaches, let him/her proclaim Jesus Christ (Colossians 1:28). Let my pastor's preaching be in the energy of the Holy Spirit.

21. Lord, by Your Holy Spirit, anoint _____ to preach, and bring apostolic results (Acts 2:37). As my pastor speaks the Word, let signs and wonders follow confirming it (Mark 16:20). Let the sick be healed; let the oppressed be set free. Anoint _____ with the truth (Matthew 16:17). Let people be cut to the heart and accept Jesus Christ.

22. Lord, as You have promised, grant my beloved shepherd lasting fruit (Malachi 3:11, John 15:16). Let my pastor's converts become disciples who in turn disciple. Bless my pastor with disciples who grow in the grace and knowledge of Jesus Christ.

23. Lord, keep my pastor in the fear of God. Let my pastor not fear people (Proverbs 19:23). Give _____ boldness to confront sin and church controllers. Honor my pastor's stand for You. Come to my pastor's rescue. I claim Psalm 35 for my shepherd.

24. O God, allow _____ to enter Your rest (Hebrews 4, Matthew 11:28). Put Your yoke on my pastor. When my pastor is heavily laden or burdened, may he/she find comfort and peace in You, refreshed and renewed by Your power in every aspect of his/her life.

Formerly a fulltime pastor, TERRY TEKYL now heads Renewal Ministries. This article is taken from *Pray!*, Issue 2, pp. 32-34. It is adapted from *Preyed On or Prayed For: Hedging Your Pastor in Prayer* (there are 40 Scripture-based prayers in the book) © 1994 by Terry Tekyl. Published by Prayer Point Press. Used by permission. To order call, 1-888-656-6067. To order copies of this article (as a bookmark prayer guide or as a desktop perpetual calendar) call 1-800-366-7788, or go to www.praymag.com.

November

saying "thank you"

"In humility we acknowledge God's majesty, in contentment His grace, and in thankfulness His goodness. Thankfulness to God is a recognition that God in His goodness and faithfulness has provided for us and cared for us, both physically and spiritually. It is a recognition that we are totally dependent upon Him; that all that we are and have comes from God . . . To fail to be thankful to God is a most grievous sin."

—Jerry Bridges

Jerry Bridges, *The Practice of Godliness* (Colorado Springs, CO: NavPress, 2001), p. 100.

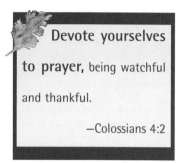

> **Devote yourselves to prayer,** being watchful and thankful.
>
> —Colossians 4:2

november 1 · Ezekiel 20-23, Psalm 123-124

november 2 · Ezekiel 24-26, Psalm 125

An Attitude of Gratitude

Thankfulness means "to express gratitude." Sometimes we feel glad because someone did something nice, but we never get around to telling that person. Thankfulness is being so full of thanks that we can't keep it inside! We just have to tell God "thank You" or we'll burst!

november 3 · Ezekiel 27-30, Psalm 126

november 4 · Ezekiel 31-34, Psalm 127

november 5 · Ezekiel 35-39, Psalm 128

november 6 · Ezekiel 40-42, Psalm 129

Sometimes people confuse praising God with thanking Him. What's the difference? When we praise God, we celebrate Him for who He is. When we thank God, we celebrate Him for what He does. For instance, we praise God because He is love. We thank Him for loving us so much that He sent Jesus!

When we pray, let's be sure to have an attitude of gratitude, praising God for who He is, and thanking Him for what He's done and is doing, and what He has promised to do.

—Sandra Higley
(*Pray*Kids!, p. 1, *Pray!*
Issue 26, p.21.)

> **You are my God, and I will give you** thanks; you are my God, and I will exalt you. Give thanks to the LORD, for he is good; his love endures forever.
>
> —Psalm 118:28,29

november 7 · *Reflection*

november 8 · Ezekiel 43–45, Psalm 130–131

november 9 · Ezekiel 46–48, Psalm 132

Trustful Thanks

Trust means going ahead and saying thanks when you don't feel like it. Trustful thanks is based on God's nature and not on our feelings. Thanking God during good times is a natural response; but thanking Him in a difficult situation is an act of the

november 10 · John 1-3, Psalm 133-134

november 11 · John 4-6, Psalm 135

november 12 · John 7-9, Psalm 136

will. I'm impressed with the lesson one intercessor friend shared with me about trustful thanks.

"If I had a flat tire, I would thank God that it was in my driveway rather than on some deserted stretch of road or that it hadn't been a blowout on the highway. But God started convicting me that I was thanking Him around the situation—not for the situation itself.

"He pointed out that He would not have permitted these particular situations unless they could perfect me. They were refining fire. They actually were answers to prayers, for I had been praying for a deeper walk and to be a purer vessel. So rather than thanking God for not allowing the trouble to be worse than it was, I began thanking Him for the trouble itself."

—Brenda Poinsett

(*Pray!*, Issue 31, p. 39.)

> **Be joyful always;**
> pray continually; give
> thanks in all circumstances,
> for this is God's will for you
> in Christ Jesus.
>
> —1 Thessalonians 5:16-18

november 13 · John 10-12, Psalm 137

november 14 · *Reflection*

in ALL circumstances

Praying during times of tragedy can be difficult. Sometimes we just don't know how to pray. And that's when we take comfort that the Holy Spirit intercedes on our behalf "with groans that

november 15 · John 13-15, Psalm 138

november 16 • John 16-18, Psalm 139

november 17 • John 19-21, Psalm 140

november 18 • Daniel 1-3, Psalm 141

words cannot express" (Romans 8:26). How might we thank God during difficult times?

We can thank God that the enemy has made a tactical error, since God will use for good what Satan has intended for harm (Genesis 50:20-21). Thank Him for the people who will be drawn to seek God's face because the overwhelming nature of the tragedy leaves them nowhere else to turn (John 2:1-9).

Thank God for a vivid reminder of your own mortality and vulnerability, asking Him to prepare your heart and spirit for a faithful response when you are faced with tragedy.

—Lani Hinkle
and Sandra Higley
(*Pray!*, Issue 27, p. 51.)

> **Let them give thanks to the LORD** for his unfailing love and his wonderful deeds for men, for he satisfies the thirsty and fills the hungry with good things.
>
> —Psalm 107:8,9

november 19 • Daniel 4-6, Psalm 142

november 20 • Daniel 7-9, Psalm 143

HOLiday Thankfulness

Every Thanksgiving, our family heads outdoors for a walk and a talk with God. As we walk beside each other, we express our thanks to God. We usually designate a place to begin: "When

november 21 • *Reflection*

november 22 · Daniel 10-12, Psalm 144

november 23 · 1 Thessalonians 1-2, Psalm 145

november 24 · 1 Thessalonians 3-5, Psalm 146

we get to the top of the hill, Bob, will you start our prayer time?" And we always designate a place to end: "I'll conclude our thanks when we get to the railroad."

At the designated starting place, my husband begins, "Good morning, Heavenly Father, our family wants to express our gratitude to You. I will begin by thanking You for _____. Your kindness has been a blessing to me." Then I pray. I thank God for something specific, followed by our children in birth order.

When each of us has covered the things we want to mention to God, we say, "I pass." Why not encourage your family to go for a walk and talk with God this week?

—Brenda Poinsett
(*Pray!*, Issue 33, p. 11.)

> **Therefore, since we are surrounded** by such a great cloud of witnesses, let us throw off everything that hinders and the sin that so easily entangles, and let us run with perseverance the race marked out for us. Let us fix our eyes on Jesus, the author and perfecter of our faith, who for the joy set before him endured the cross, scorning its shame, and sat down at the right hand of the throne of God. Consider him who endured such opposition from sinful men, so that you will not grow weary and lose heart.
>
> —Hebrews 12:1-3

november 25 · Joel, Psalm 147

november 26 · Micah 1-3, Psalm 148

november 27 · Micah 4-5, Psalm 149

november 28 · Micah 6-7, Psalm 150

_____
_____
_____
_____
_____
_____
_____
_____
_____
_____
_____

november 29 · _Reflection_

_____
_____
_____
_____
_____
_____
_____
_____
_____
_____
_____

november 30 · _Reflection_

_____
_____
_____
_____
_____
_____
_____
_____
_____
_____
_____

Heaven's cake

If Jesus were the only gift God ever gave, would you be thankful?

Mother Teresa said once, "Jesus is not all you need until He is all you have." She also said, "Perhaps God's judgment on America today is the plague of _muchness._"

If we have so much, we tend not to be thankful for Jesus. And if we are not thankful for Jesus, we tend not to be thankful for everything else. Because if we are truly thankful for Jesus, if we are genuinely gripped by all that He accomplished for us, then everything else is just icing on the cake. The cake is Jesus!

What did Jesus do? Throughout this week ponder these passages: Philippians 2:5-11, Ephesians 2:1-7, and Colossians 1:15-22. What would our thankfulness look like if these thoughts were always filling our minds?

—Vic Black
Prayer Ministry Coordinator,
The Navigators

notes

monthLy RefLection

What is the Spirit of God saying to me this month? What is my response?

prayer for the month:

Thank You, God of gods—You are good! Thank You, Lord of lords—Your love lasts forever! I acknowledge that everything I have comes from You. I don't have anything to
offer back to You that didn't come directly from Your hand. I choose to be joyful and
give thanks no matter what—free from anxiety. Along with my thanks I give You praise,
glory, wisdom, honor, power and strength forever and ever (Psalm 136:1-3; 1 Chronicles
29:14; 1 Thessalonians 5:16-18; Philippians 4:6; Revelation 7:12).

prayers of Hope in times of calamity

By Cynthia Hyle Bezek

Tragedies come in all sizes and forms. They range from malicious, premeditated tragedies (like a large-scale terrorist attack or violent murder) to unavoidable but equally devastating tragedies that affect communities or individuals (such as fires and floods, cancer and car wrecks). Naturally, how you pray will depend on the specific crisis. There are, however, some common denominators that apply to any calamity. People who hurt need hope; they need an eternal perspective; they need others to reach out and care for them; they need to reach out to the Father and trust Him. As you pray for the people involved in a calamity or crisis, adapt these Scripture-based prayers as the Holy Spirit leads.

1. Dear Lord, if these hurting people have not called on You before, may they begin calling on Your name right now; may they find You to be their refuge and strength, an ever-present help in their time of trouble (Genesis 4:26; Psalm 46:1).

2. Lord of heaven and earth, encourage these friends to seek You, reach out to You, and find You because You are not far from them. Give them hope that You are with them so that the waters they are passing through will not sweep them away, and the fire they are walking through will not burn them (Acts 17:27; Isaiah 43:2).

3. Living Word, make Your Word come alive to those who suffer. When their souls are weary with sorrow, strengthen them according to Your Word. Give them longing for Your precepts, and preserve their lives by them. Comfort them with Your promises. Use this affliction to bring them near to Your ways. Sustain them according to Your promise, and do not let their hopes be dashed. Give them a love for Your law, Lord, so they will have great peace and nothing will cause them to stumble (Psalm 119:28,40,50,67,116,165).

4. God of peace and unity, bind affected families together in love. When one member is weak, fill the others with strength and compassion so that the one who falls will have someone to pick him up. Help them not to lose patience with each other, attack each other, or in any other way be separated by these tragic circumstances; instead, knit them together in love and strength (Ecclesiastes 4:9-12; Matthew 19:6).

5. Loving Father, draw the children involved in this tragedy to Yourself. Let them come to You without hindrance. Strip away any foothold in their lives that Satan may try to gain through this tragedy. Rather, use it to refine their faith in You (Matthew 19:13-14; Luke 17:1-2; Ephesians 1:27; 1 Peter 1:6-7).

6. Stir Your body to action, Lord Jesus. Surround these hurting people with those who will minister to them. Send believers who will offer food, visits, and other ministry in Your Name. Prompt Your people to reach out and offer the comfort they themselves have received from You. Give them opportunities to share the reason for the hope they have (Matthew 25:37-40; 2 Corinthians 1:3-4; 1 Peter 3:15).

7. Eternal Father, prompt these friends to view their circumstances from the perspective of eternity. Help them to consider the fleetingness of life, the vain bustling around, and the storing up of wealth. Cause them to ponder the eternity You have set in their hearts. Give them a heart of wisdom as they realize that all our days are numbered (Psalm 39:4-6; Ecclesiastes 3:11; Psalm 90:10-12).

8. Sovereign Lord, help these dear ones to be like Job, to see You as good and find reasons to praise You even though You have taken away. Grant them faith to accept trouble from You as well as good things, and give them confidence that even though You slay them, they can still hope in You (Job 1:21, 2:10, 13:15).

9. Great Redeemer, protect these friends from feeling persecuted. Bless them with confidence that You intend good

for them. Please redeem every loss and every painful memory, and use them for the saving of many lives. Help them to know that You understand how they feel because You also suffered (Genesis 50:20; Hebrews 4:15-16).

10. Author of life, on behalf of these friends I come before You to resist every attempt of the evil one to steal and kill and destroy through this tragedy. You are the resurrection and the life; bring the blessings of life and fullness into these friends' lives (John 10:10, 11:25).

11. Merciful Savior, help these friends to see Your grace clearly and seek it to guard themselves against any root of bitterness (Hebrews 12:15).

12. God of all hope, help these friends to not lose sight of the plans You have for them—to prosper them and not to harm them, to give them a hope and a future. Help them, Holy Spirit, to hope in You and not in circumstances, so their strength will be renewed. Fill them with joy and peace as they trust in You so that they may overflow with hope by the power of the Holy Spirit (Jeremiah 29:11; Isaiah 40:31; Romans 15:13).

CYNTHIA BEZEK is the managing editor of *Pray!*. To order this article as a full-color bookmark prayer guide, (50 per pack), call 1-800-366-7788 and ask for item #239, or go to www.praymag.com.

December

Abiding in Him

"Prayer is welcoming our Father's presence into a lifetime conversation with our hearts. Calling Him up throughout the hour, day, week, month, year of our lives like calling up your best friend, or your father or mother, or the person you love most in the world. Finally, prayer is our ultimate conversation of knowing and being known, of loving and being loved. This communion with our Father sustains us for this lifetime and whets our appetites for the next."

—Dudley J. Delffs

Dudley J. Delffs, *The Prayer Centered Life* (Colorado Springs, CO: NavPress, 1997), p. 186.

> **And they were calling to one another:** "Holy, holy, holy is the LORD Almighty; the whole earth is full of his glory."
>
> —Isaiah 6:3

december 1 · 2 Thessalonians, Isaiah 40

december 2 · Nahum, Isaiah 41

HOLY, HOLY, HOLY

Imagine the multiple-winged seraphs covering their faces because they cannot possibly take in so much of God—the overwhelming nature of His beauty, His character, and His holiness. Like these celestial beings of the Bible, we also have been given an invitation by God to draw near to Him (James 4:8).

december 3 · 2 Peter, Isaiah 42

december 4 · Habakkuk, Isaiah 43

december 5 · Zephaniah, Isaiah 44

december 6 · Jude, Isaiah 45

God wants to reveal Himself to each of us individually (Ephesians 1:17-18).

We certainly will go through "cold" seasons where the tingles fade and the burning dwindles in our relationship with the Lord. These are the moments when we must pursue intimacy with and revelation from God. Then, as our hearts start to flicker again, we find a solitary place and pray the Scriptures to ignite the flame.

We don't have to wait for heaven to experience intimacy with God. It's available to us now through the Holy Spirit, the Scriptures, and prayer. So let's draw as close as we possibly can to the heart of God this side of heaven!

—David Perkins
(*Pray!*, Issue 37, p. 15.)

> **Awake, awake!**
> Clothe yourself with strength, O arm of the LORD; awake, as in days gone by, as in generations of old.
>
> —Isaiah 51:9

december 7 · *Reflection*

december 8 · Haggai, Isaiah 46–47

december 9 · Zechariah 1–3, Isaiah 48

Great Awakening

Scripture portrays revival as a spiritual "awakening" to Christ and all that He is. We experience a foretaste of it every morning as we awaken to the day and get out of bed. My first prayer for awakening is Isaiah 51:9a. I pray for *God* to wake up!

december 10 · Zechariah 4-6, Isaiah 49

december 11 · Zechariah 7-9, Isaiah 50

december 12 · Zechariah 10-12, Isaiah 51

Isaiah says that when the Spirit goes into action in powerful new ways, it almost feels, by contrast, as if a moment earlier He had been sleeping. But when God wakes up, then His people wake up. When Christ shines, we can rise—and the world around us!

Even wise virgins may fall asleep (Matthew 25:1-13), but not for long. The Bridegroom is on His way for arrival, for awakening. He is the sunrise *before* our prayers, and *for* our prayers. Who wants to sleep through that?

—David Bryant
(*Pray!*, Issue 31, p. 7.)

> I urge, then, first of all, that requests, prayers, intercession and thanksgiving be made for everyone.
>
> —1 Timothy 2:1

december 13 · Zechariah 13-14, Isaiah 52-53

december 14 · *Reflection*

pray all day

From the moment you get up in the morning to the moment you drift off to sleep once again, you'll notice that prayer needs are ever before you! Here's how the Lord's leading me to be devoted to prayer:

• At 7:30 a.m., a school bus passes my house. I usually see it

december 15 · Malachi 1-2, Isaiah 54

december 16 • Malachi 3-4, Isaiah 55

december 17 • Revelation 1-2, Isaiah 56

december 18 • Revelation 3-4, Isaiah 57

while I'm exercising. It reminds me to pray for students, teachers, and other school employees.

• Whenever I hear a siren or see an emergency vehicle, I pray for those who are in pain or danger. I pray for wisdom for their caregivers.

• At the grocery store, I pray for people I see. As I fill my basket, I pray for the less fortunate.

• When I pass a hospital, nursing home, school, factory, church, or other place where people are gathered, I pray.

• As I listen to the nightly news, prayer needs abound!

—Loretta Wadsworth
(*Pray!*, Issue 10, p. 11.)

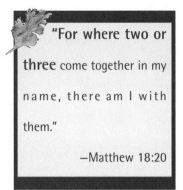

> "For where two or three come together in my name, there am I with them."
>
> —Matthew 18:20

december 19 • Revelation 5-6, Isaiah 58

december 20 • Revelation 7-8, Isaiah 59

come together

A wave of united prayer is surging around the globe in our day. More Christians are praying than ever before. The increase in numbers is a gratifying surprise, but the outstanding feature of today's prayer movement is that we are finding ways to pray together.

Perhaps you've experienced the joy of an abiding relationship

december 21 • *Reflection*

december 22 · Revelation 9-10, Isaiah 60

december 23 · Revelation 11-12, Isaiah 61

december 24 · Revelation 13-14, Isaiah 62

with the Lord through prayer, and now God is calling you to walk alongside and pray with others. Here are some ways to make that happen:

• Ask your pastor how you can help develop prayer within your church.

• Find at least one person you can pray with weekly. Make revival in your life, your church, and your country the main focus of your prayer time.

• Take part in community and national prayer events, be it a March for Jesus, a community-wide concert of prayer, or a prayer breakfast. Pray with those from other churches and denominations.

—Steve Hawthorne and *Pray!*
(*Pray!*, Issue 1, pp. 18-19.)

> "I am the true vine, and my Father is the gardener. He cuts off every branch in me that bears no fruit, while every branch that does bear fruit he prunes so that it will be even more fruitful."
>
> —John 15:1,2

december 25 · Revelation 15-16, Isaiah 63

december 26 · Revelation 17-18, Isaiah 64

december 27 · Revelation 19-20, Isaiah 65

the fruitful branch

We're introduced to the greatest gardener of all in John 15. Every good gardener knows you have to prune your plants and trees to get maximum yield. And so with God.

december 28 · Revelation 21–22, Isaiah 66

december 29 · *Reflection*

december 30 · *Reflection*

Notice two things here. First, there is a severity in this picture of God. And second, there is a single-mindedness in this picture of God.

As a gardener, God has one interest—that the branches bear lots of fruit. If He doesn't find any, Jesus says He takes that branch away. And every branch that bears fruit He prunes to bring more fruit. God takes whatever action is necessary to cleanse His people so they will produce fruit for His glory.

The key to it all is that the people of God must abide in—live in close, day-by-day fellowship with—Jesus Christ.

—Leroy Eims
(Excerpted from *Daily Discipleship* by LeRoy Eims © 1998. Used by permission of NavPress [www.navpress.com]. All rights reserved.)

december 31 · *Reflection*

monthly reflection

What is the Spirit of God saying to me this month? What is my response?

prayer for the month:

Lord, teach me to abide in You. I want to learn to stay in Your shelter so that I can rest in Your shadow. One day in Your courts is better than a thousand days anywhere else. If I can't go with You, Father, I don't want to go at all. Your path is the only one worth taking. Thank You for making it known to me. Fill me with joy in Your presence (John15:4; Psalms 91:1, 84:10; Exodus 33:15; Psalm 16:11).

12 prayers for christmas

By Sandra Higley

Christmas is a glorious time of year! God brings us face to face once again with His design for and redemption of mankind. His intentions toward us are for life lived abundantly. His plans for the kingdom are victorious!

But for many people, the holidays can be filled with unrealistic expectations. Old hurts are sometimes revisited and new ones inflicted. Hope can go deferred and result in heartsickness (Proverbs 13:12). In the midst of the tinsel and lights and shopping, let's remember what the season is really about! Let's pray for a spirit of *all things Christmas* for ourselves and our loved ones.

1. LOVE. Lord, help us follow the way of love—let the love of Christ compel us (1 Corinthians 14:1; 2 Corinthians 5:14).

2. JOY. Restore the joy of Your salvation to us; let us experience the joy of Your presence (Psalm 51:12, 16:11).

3. PEACE. Let Your peace rule and guard our hearts; give us more of You—You are our peace (Colossians 3:15; Philippians 4:7; Ephesians 2:14).

4. HOPE. Enlighten the eyes of our heart so that we may know the hope You called us to (Ephesians 1:18).

5. FAVOR. Let Your favor rest on us (Luke 2:52).

6. LIFE. Shine Your light of life on us; help us to walk in it (Job 33:30; Psalm 56:13).

7. SALVATION. Help us to fear You so we can unlock the treasure of Your salvation (Isaiah 33:6).

8. SELFLESSNESS. Keep us from self-seeking attitudes that reject truth (Romans 2:8).

9. GENEROSITY. Make us rich in ways that result in generosity on our part so You will be praised (2 Corinthians 9:11).

10. RECEIVING. Help us receive Your kingdom, Your Spirit, and Your grace (Daniel 7:18; John 20:22; Romans 5:17).

11. SEEKING. Encourage us to seek Your face with all our hearts (Deuteronomy 4:29; Psalm 27:8).

12. PRAISE. We ascribe glory to Your name, Lord; we come before You in worship for You are holy (1 Chronicles 16:28-29).

SANDRA HIGLEY is the assistant editor of *Pray!*.

answered prayers

"I will praise you, O Lᴏʀᴅ, with all my heart;

before the 'gods' I will sing your praise.

I will bow down toward your holy temple and will praise your name

for your love and your faithfulness,

for you have exalted above all things your name and your word.

When I called, you answered me."

—Psalm 138:1-3

Date Prayed	Date Answered	God's Response
_____	_____	_____
_____	_____	_____
_____	_____	_____
_____	_____	_____
_____	_____	_____
_____	_____	_____
_____	_____	_____
_____	_____	_____
_____	_____	_____
_____	_____	_____
_____	_____	_____
_____	_____	_____
_____	_____	_____
_____	_____	_____
_____	_____	_____
_____	_____	_____

Date Prayed	Date Answered	God's Response

Date Prayed	Date Answered	God's Response

continuing the journey

Helps and Resources to Keep You Praying

"I am the vine; you are the branches.

If a man remains in me and I in him, he will bear much fruit;

apart from me you can do nothing."

—John 15:5

maintaining a weLL-BaLanced prayer Life

The Navigators has always been known as a ministry of prayer. We live in light of the fact that we are desperately dependent upon the Lord.

Followers of Christ must remember just how vital our relationship with Him is. "I am the vine; you are the branches," Jesus said. "If a man remains in me and I in him, he will bear much fruit; apart from me you can do nothing" (John 15:5).

The following traditional Navigator illustration will help you get a better grasp of prayer in your day-to-day walk with God:

- Confession (1 John 1:9)—Agreeing with God about my sin
- Petition (1 Samuel 1:27) (Samuel asked of God)—Asking God for my needs
- Intercession (Ephesians 6:18,19)—Praying for others
- Thanksgiving (Ephesians 5:20)—Thanking God for what He has done for me
- Praise (Psalm 146:1,2)—Voicing my wonder about who God is
- Prayer is not only an action (work) but an attitude (1 Samuel 12:23)

As the thumb touches all four fingers, so praise should permeate my whole prayer life.

(The Navigators. Used with permission.)

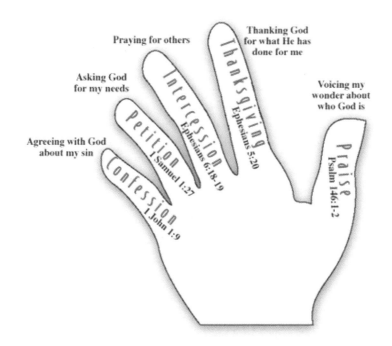

Pray on the Full Armor of God

By Dean Ridings

The person who seeks to have a vital relationship with God through prayer—ever growing toward greater intimacy with the Father through the finished work of the Son, Jesus—is a prime target for satanic salvos.

The Scriptures tell us that the enemy is bent on destruction and will do whatever it takes to leave us discouraged, doubting, and defeated Christians. In our scientific society where nothing we can't see, feel, touch, taste, or smell seems real, some scoff at the mention of a spiritual battle. The Bible, however, makes it clear: We have an "enemy the devil [who] prowls around like a roaring lion looking for someone to devour" (1 Peter 5:8).

But Jesus promises that His followers can both survive and thrive through the battle: "I have come that they may have life, and have it to the full" (John 10:10).

Satan Has a Terrible Plan

To get an idea of the activities of the devil and his fallen-angel followers, just look at the names for them throughout Scripture. Among many descriptive titles, the devil is called the wicked one, adversary, father of lies. Fallen angels are called evil spirits, demons, unclean spirits. Together, their expressed activities include:

• tempting (Matthew 4:1)
• lying (John 8:44)
• accusing (Zechariah 3:1)
• corrupting (2 Peter 2:10-12)
• deceiving (1 Timothy 4:1)

We must realize that Jesus' death on the cross sealed the final judgment of demonic forces: "When He had disarmed the rulers and authorities, He made a public display of them, having triumphed over them through Him" (Colossians 2:15; see also John 16:11,19:30; Hebrews 2:14).

Yet the enemy and his followers are in denial. They still operate as if victory is within their grasp. They continue to do whatever they can to affect humankind—made in the image of God and with the potential of glorifying and being glorified by Him.

Though the ultimate war has been won, we are engaged in a daily battle against the prince of this world. We are clearly warned in God's word of the damage that can be inflicted by the kingdom of darkness. The enemy schemes against us, throws flaming missiles at us, seeks to devour us, and wages direct warfare upon us (2 Corinthians 2:10,11; Ephesians 6:11,12,16; 1 Peter 5:8). As a result, we are to arm ourselves, stand against, refute, resist, and overcome (Ephesians 6:12-18; Isaiah 54:7; James 4:7; Revelation 12:11). Everything we need to successfully do battle was provided for us on the cross. We simply need to appropriate it.

How Should We Then Live?

Here are three Scripture-based suggestions to help you live in light of the spiritual reality that demonic forces are at work to hinder your prayer life, spiritual growth, and effectiveness for eternity's sake.

Prepare Your Heart. Personal preparation begins with the psalmist's prayer, "Search me, O God, and know my heart; test me and know my anxious thoughts. See if there is any offensive way in me, and lead me in the way everlasting" (Psalm 139:23-24).

Praise and Worship God. Praise and worship means turning your heart toward God—focusing on His attributes, thanking Him for who He is, what He has done, and what He is going to do. Singing is an important part of praise and worship, just as psalmwriter David said: "I will praise God's name in song and glorify him with thanksgiving. This will please the LORD more than [sacrifices]" (Psalm 69:30-31). Praise and worship are powerful forms of spiritual warfare (2 Chronicles 20:22; Psalm 8:2).

Pray. Prayer is crucial in battling Satan and his demons. Among the pieces of defensive spiritual armor, God has given His children two offensive pieces as well: the Sword of the Spirit (God's word), and prayer (Ephesians 6:10-18).

The following prayer, based on that passage, is offered to help you get in the habit of praying on the armor of God each day—each morning, in fact, at the outset of your quiet time with God. Adapt it, make it your own, and pray in faith that the Lord not only hears your prayer but prepares you to experience His victory today.

Daily Victory Prayer
Based on Ephesians 6:10-18

Lord, I'm reminded that my "struggle is not against flesh and blood, but against the rulers, against the authorities, against the powers of this dark world and against the spiritual forces of evil in the heavenly realms."

Therefore, I pray that You will once again equip me with the full armor of God, so that when evil comes, I may be able to stand my ground. Equip me, Lord:

• With the belt of truth. May Your truth rule in my heart and be in my mind and on my lips today.

• With the breastplate of righteousness. Apart from You there is no righteousness, but through Jesus I have been "born again" and made righteous in Your sight. May I live as a righteous person.

• With feet fitted with the readiness that comes from the Gospel of peace. May I reflect the Gospel in my words and actions, that through me, with my every encounter, others may be drawn "one step closer" to You.

• With the shield of faith. May I take You at Your word concerning promises about the present and future—promises of everlasting love, abundant life, and so forth.

• With the helmet of salvation. Remind me that nothing can separate me from Your love, that by grace I've been saved. In Your grace help me to say "no" to all ungodliness and worldly passions, and to live a self-controlled, upright, and godly life.

• And with the sword of the Spirit, the Word of God. May Your Holy Spirit reign in my life and bring to my mind just the right Bible verses to be in my heart and on my lips; may I be "filled with the Spirit" and ready with Scripture as You were, Jesus, when the devil tried to tempt You.

• Finally, keep me in an attitude of prayer. May I "practice the presence of God" throughout the day. May I "pray in the Spirit on all occasions with all kinds of prayers and requests."

Thank You that You hear the prayers of Your people, and that I am Your child. Help me to be Your person in this world today—salt and light, moment by moment. In Jesus' name. Amen.

Based upon "Understanding the Essentials of Spiritual Warfare" by Dean Ridings, © 1997, 1999, 2001 by CCI/USA. Excerpted and adapted with permission.

HOW to spend a Day in Prayer

By Lorne Sanny

Biola College student Lorne Sanny's life was never the same after meeting Navigator founder Dawson Trotman at an early-morning campus Bible club. Discipled by "Daws," Lorne joined Nav staff in 1941.

And after Dawson's untimely death in 1956, for the next three decades Lorne served as The Navigators' second president and chairman of the board.

A centerpiece of Lorne's legacy is prayer, and in this enduring piece he outlines how each follower of Jesus can spend a vibrant day in prayer. Why not set aside a day a month, a quarter, or perhaps at the end of this or beginning of next year in prayer?

"Prayer is a powerful thing, for God has bound and tied Himself thereto."

—Martin Luther

"God's acquaintance is not made hurriedly. He does not bestow His gifts on the casual or hasty comer and goer. To be much alone with God is the secret of knowing Him and of influence with Him."

—E. M. Bounds

"I never thought a day could make such a difference," a friend said to me. "My relationship to everyone seems improved."

"Why don't I do it more often?" another friend commented.

Comments like these come from those who set aside a personal day of prayer.

With so many activities—important ones—clamoring for our time, real prayer is considered more a luxury than a necessity. How much more so spending a day in prayer!

The Bible gives us three time-guides for personal prayer. There is the command to "pray without ceasing"—the spirit of prayer—keeping so in time with God that we can lift our hearts in request or praise anytime through the day.

There is also the practice of a quiet time or morning watch—seen in the life of David (Psalm 5:3), or Daniel (6:10), and of the Lord Jesus (Mark 1:35). This daily time specified for meditation in the Word of God and prayer is indispensable to the growing,

healthy Christian.

Then there are examples in the Scripture of extended time given to prayer alone. Jesus spent whole nights praying. Nehemiah prayed "certain days" upon hearing of the plight of Jerusalem. Three times Moses spent 40 days and 40 nights alone with God.

Learning from God

I believe it was in these special times of prayer that God made known His ways and His plans to Moses (Psalm 103:7). He allowed Moses to look through a chink in the fence and gain special insights, while the rank and file Israelites saw only the acts of God as they unfolded day by day.

Once I remarked to Dawson Trotman, founder of The Navigators, "You impress me as one who feels he is a man of destiny, one destined to be used of God."

"I don't think that's the case," he replied, "but I know this. God has given me some promises that I know He will fulfill." During earlier years Daws spent countless protracted times alone with God, and out of these times the Navigator work grew—not by methods or principles, but by promises given to him through the Word.

In my own life, one of the most refreshing and stabilizing factors, as well as the means for new direction or confirmation of the will of God, has been those extended times of prayer—in the neighborhood park in Seattle, on a hill behind the Navigator home in Southern California, or out in the Garden of the Gods in Colorado Springs.

These special prayer times can become anchor points in your life, times when you "drive a stake" as a landmark and go on from there. Your daily quiet time is more effective as you pray into day-by-day reality some of the things the Lord speaks to your heart in protracted times of prayer. The quiet time in turn is the foundation for "praying without ceasing," going through the day in communion with God.

Perhaps you haven't spent a protracted time in prayer because you haven't recognized the need for it. Or maybe you aren't sure what you would do with a whole day on your hands *just to pray.*

why a Day in Prayer?

Why take this time from a busy life? What is it for?

1. For extended fellowship with God—beyond your morning devotions. It means just plain being with and thinking about God. God has called us into the fellowship of His Son, Jesus Christ (1 Corinthians 1:9). Like many personal relationships, this fellowship is nurtured by spending time together. God takes special note of times when His people reverence Him and *think upon His Name* (Malachi 3:16).

2. For a renewed perspective. Like flying over the battlefield in a reconnaissance plane, a day of prayer gives opportunity to think of the world from God's point of view. Especially when going through some difficulty, we need this perspective to sharpen our vision of the unseen, and to let the immediate, tangible things drop into proper place. Our spiritual defenses are strengthened while "we fix our eyes not on what is seen, but on what is unseen. For ... what is unseen is eternal" (2 Corinthians 4:18).

3. For prayerful consideration of our own lives before the Lord—personal inventory and evaluation. You will especially want to take a day of prayer when facing important decisions, as well as on a periodic basis. On such a day you can evaluate where you are in relation to your goals and get direction from the Lord through His Word. Promises are there for you and me, just as they have been for Hudson Taylor or George Mueller or Dawson Trotman. And it is in our times alone with God that He gives inner assurance of His promises to us.

4. For adequate preparation. Nehemiah, after spending "certain days" seeking the Lord in prayer, was called in before the king. "Then the king said unto me, 'For what dost thou make request?' So I prayed to the God of heaven. And I said unto the king, 'If it please the king ... '"—and he outlined his plan (Nehemiah 2:4,5, KJV). Then Nehemiah says, "I arose in the night, I and some few men with me; neither told I any man what my God had put in my heart to do at Jerusalem" (2:12). When did God put in his heart this plan? I believe it was when he fasted and prayed and waited on God. Then when the day came for action, he was ready.

I heard a boy ask a pilot if it didn't take quick thinking to land his plane when something went wrong. The pilot answered that no, he knew at all times where he would put down if something went wrong. He had that thought out ahead of time.

So it should be in our Christian life. If God has given us plans and purposes in those times alone, we will be ready when opportunity comes to move right into it. We won't have to say, "I'm not prepared." The reason many Christians are dead to opportunities is not because they are not mentally alert, but they are simply unprepared in heart. Preparation is made when we get alone with God.

pray on the Basis of God's word

Daniel said, "In the first year of [Darius'] reign I, Daniel, understood from the Scriptures, according to the word of the LORD given to Jeremiah the prophet, that the desolation of Jerusalem would last 70 years. So I turned to the Lord God and pleaded with Him in prayer and petition, in fasting, and in sackcloth and ashes. I prayed to the LORD my God and confessed" (Daniel 9:2-4).

He understood by the Scriptures what was to come. And as a result of his exposure to the Word of God, he prayed. It has been said that God purposes, therefore He promises. And we can add, "Therefore I pray the promises, so that God's purposes might come to reality." God purposed to do something, and He promised it, therefore, Daniel prayed. This was Daniel's part in completing the circuit, like an electrical circuit, so that the power could flow through.

Your day alone with the Lord isn't a matter of sitting out on a rock like the statue of *The Thinker* and taking whatever thoughts come to your mind. That's not safe. It should be a day exposed to God's Word, and then His Word leads you into prayer. You will end the day worse than you started if all you do is engage in introspection, thinking of yourself and your own problems. It isn't your estimate of yourself that counts anyway. It's God's estimate. And He will reveal His estimate to you by the Holy Spirit through His Word, the open Bible. And then the Word leads into prayer.

Find a Place Away

How do you go about it? Having set aside a day or portion of a day for prayer, pack a lunch and start out. Find a place where you can be alone, away from distractions. This may be a wooded area near home or your backyard. An outdoor spot is excellent if you can find it, but don't get sidetracked into nature studies and fritter away your time. If you find yourself watching the squirrels or the ants, direct your observation by reading Psalm 104 and meditating on the power of God in creation.

Take along a Bible, a notebook and pencil, a chorus or hymn book, and perhaps a devotional book. I like to have with me the booklet *Power Through Prayer* by E. M. Bounds and read a chapter or two as a challenge to the strategic value of prayer. Or I sometimes take Horatius Bonar's *Words to Winners of Souls,* or a missionary biography like *Behind the Ranges* by Mary C. Taylor, which records the prayer victories of J. O. Fraser in inland China.

Even if you have all day, you will want to use it profitably. So lose no time in starting, and start purposefully.

wait on the Lord

Divide the day into three parts: waiting on the Lord, prayer for others, and prayer for yourself.

As you *wait on the Lord,* don't hurry. You will miss the point if you look for some mystical or ecstatic experience. Just seek the Lord, waiting on *Him.* Isaiah 40:3 promises that those who wait upon the Lord will renew their strength. Psalm 27:14 is one of dozens of verses that mention waiting on Him as is Psalm 62:5, "Find rest, O my soul, in God alone; my hope comes from Him."

Wait on Him first *to realize His presence.* Read through a passage like Psalm 139, grasping the truth of His presence with you as you read each verse. Ponder the impossibility of being anywhere in the universe where He is not. Often we are like Jacob when he said, "Surely the Lord is in this place; and I knew it not" (Genesis 28:16, KJV).

Wait on Him also *for cleansing.* The last two verses of Psalm 139 lead you into this. Ask God to search your heart as these verses suggest. When we search our own hearts, it can lead to imaginations, morbid introspection, or anything the enemy may want to throw before us. But when the Holy Spirit searches, He will bring to your attention that which should be confessed and cleansed. Psalms 51 and 32, David's songs of confession, will help you. Stand upon the firm ground of 1 John 1:9 and claim God's faithfulness to forgive whatever specific thing you confess.

If you realize you've sinned against a brother, make a note of it so you won't forget to set it right. Otherwise, the rest of the day will be hindered. God won't be speaking to you if there is something between you and someone else that you haven't planned to take care of at the earliest possible moment.

As you wait on God, ask for the power of concentration. Bring yourself back from daydreaming.

Next, wait on God to *worship Him.* Psalms 103, 111, and 145 are wonderful portions to follow as you praise the Lord for the greatness of His power. Most of the psalms are prayers. Or turn to Revelation, chapters 4 and 5, and use them in your praise to Him. There is no better way to pray scripturally than to pray Scripture.

If you brought a chorus or hymn book, you can sing to the Lord. Some wonderful inspirational music has been written that put into words what we could scarcely express ourselves. Maybe you don't sing very well—then be sure you're out of earshot of someone else and "make a joyful noise unto the Lord"; *He* will appreciate it!

This will lead you naturally into thanksgiving. Reflect upon the wonderful things God has done for you and thank Him for these—for your own salvation and spiritual blessings, for your family, friends, and opportunities. Go beyond that which you thank the Lord for daily and take time to express appreciation to Him for countless things He's given.

pray for others

Now is the time for the unhurried, more detailed prayer for others that you don't get to ordinarily. Remember people in addition to those for whom you usually pray. Trace your way around the world, praying for people by countries.

Here are three suggestions as to what to pray.

1. Ask specific things for them. Perhaps you remember or have jotted down various needs people have mentioned. Use requests from missionary prayer letters. Pray for spiritual strength, courage, physical stamina, mental alertness, and so forth. Imagine yourself in the situations where these people are and pray accordingly.

2. Look up some of the prayers in Scripture. Pray what Paul prayed for other people in the first chapter of Philippians and Colossians, and in the first and third chapters of Ephesians. This will help you advance in your prayer from the stage of "Lord, bless so and so and help him or her do such and such."

3. Ask for others what you are praying for yourself. Desire for them what the Lord has shown *you.*

4. If you pray a certain verse or promise of Scripture for a person, you may want to put the reference by his or her name on your prayer list.

Use this verse as you pray for that person the next time. Then use it for thanksgiving as you see the Lord answer.

Prayer for Yourself

The third part of your day will be prayer for yourself. If you face an important decision, you may want to put this before prayer for others.

Again, let your prayer be ordered by Scripture and ask the Lord for understanding according to Psalm 119:18. Meditate upon verses of Scripture you have memorized or promises from the Word you have previously claimed. Reading a whole book of the Bible through, perhaps aloud, is a good idea. Consider how it might apply to your life.

In prayer for yourself, 1 Chronicles 4:10 is one good example to follow. Jabez prayed, "Oh that You would bless me and enlarge my territory! Let Your hand be with me, and keep me from harm so that I will be free from pain." That's prayer for your personal life, for your growth, for God's presence, and for God's protection. Jabez prayed in the will of God, and God granted his request.

"Lord, what do *You* think of my life?" is the attitude of this portion of your day of prayer. Consider your main objectives in the light of what you know to be God's will for you. Jesus said, "My food is to do the will of Him who sent Me and to finish His work" (John 4:34). Do you want to do God's will more than anything else? Is it really your highest desire?

Then consider your activities—what you *do*—in the context of your objectives. God may speak to you about rearranging your schedule, cutting out certain activities that are good but not best or some things that are entanglements or impediments to progress. Strip them off. You may be convicted about how you spend your evenings or Saturdays, when you could use the time to advantage and still get the recreation you need.

As you pray, record your thoughts on your activities and use of time, and plan for better scheduling. Perhaps the need for better preparation for your Sunday school class or a personal visit with an individual will come to your mind. Or the Lord may impress you to do something special for someone. Make a note of it.

During this part of your day, bring up any problems or decisions you are facing and seek the mind of God on them. It helps to list the factors involved in these decisions or problems. Pray over these fac-

tors and look into the Scriptures for guidance. You may be led to a promise or direction from the passages with which you have already filled your mind during the day.

After prayer, you may reach some definite conclusions upon which you can base firm convictions. It should be your aim in a day of prayer to come away with some conclusions and specific direction—some stakes driven. However, do not be discouraged if this is not the case. It may not be God's time for a conclusive answer to your problem. And you may discover that your real need was not to know the next step but to have a new revelation of God Himself.

In looking for promises to claim, there's no need to thumb through looking for new or startling ones. Just start with the promises you already know. If you have been through the *Topical Memory System* (NavPress), start by meditating on the verses in the "Rely on God's Resources" section. Chew over some old familiar promises the Lord has given you before, ones you consider as you think back. Pray about applying these verses to your life.

I have found some of the greatest blessings from a new realization of promises I already knew. And the familiar promises may lead you to others. The Bible is full of them.

You may want to mark or underline in your Bible the promises the Lord gives during these protracted times alone, and put the date and a word or two in the margin beside them.

Variety is important during your day of prayer. Read a while, pray for a while, then walk around. A friend of mine paces the floor of his room for his prayer time. Rather than get cramped in one position, take a walk and stretch; get some variety.

As outside things pop into your mind, simply incorporate those items into prayer. If it's some business item you must not forget, jot it down. Have you noticed how many things come to mind while you are sitting in church? It will be natural for things to occur to you and plan how you can take care of them and when. Don't just push them aside or they will plague you the rest of the day.

At the end of the day, summarize in your notebook some things God has spoken to you about. This will be profitable to refer to later.

Two Questions

The result of your day of prayer should be answers to the two questions Paul asked the Lord on the

Damascus road (Acts 22:6-10). Paul's first question was, "Who are you, Lord?" The Lord replied, "I am Jesus." You will be seeking to know Him, to find out who He is. The second question Paul asked was, "What shall I do, Lord?" The Lord answered him specifically. This should be answered or reconfirmed for you in that part of the day, when you unhurriedly seek His will for you.

Don't think you must end the day with some new discovery or extraordinary experience. Wait on God and expose yourself to His Word. Looking for a new experience or insight you can share with someone when you get back will get you off the track. True, you may gain some new insight, but often this can just take your attention from the real business. The test of such a day is not how exhilarated we are when the day is over but how it works into life tomorrow. If we have really exposed ourselves to the Word and come into contact with God, it will affect our daily life. And that is what we want.

Days of prayer don't just happen. Besides the attempts of our enemy Satan to keep us from praying, the world around us has plenty to offer to fill our time. So we have to make time. Plan ahead—the first of every month, once a quarter, or at the very least a day a year.

God bless you as you do this—and do it soon! You too will probably ask yourself, "Why not more often?"

(The Navigators. Used with permission.)

Discovering God's Prayer Plan for Your Family

By Jim Carpenter

Praying for my family has always been a great privilege. But in the last few years intercession for my loved ones has taken on a new dimension. I've begun to seek God's "prayer agenda" for each family member.

Early in each new year I get away for a prayer retreat. I spend a day or two in worship, Bible study, and prayer. And I ask the Lord how I should intercede for my family during the year ahead.

In the quietness of listening prayer, God gives me a "prayer agenda" for my wife, my two sons, my elderly mother, and even for myself. Usually this includes a promise from God's Word, or a passage of Scripture that seems particularly relevant for each one.

For example, last year I prayed through Psalm 112 every day for Andy, my older son. The Psalm is a tribute to the godly man who "fears the LORD, who finds great delight in his commands" (v. 1). The Lord brought this to mind in my January prayer retreat, and it seemed very fitting for Andy, in his last year of college.

God highlighted other passages for my younger son Zach and for my wife, Dionne. And the Lord even revealed a prayer agenda for my own life. During my retreat He underscored an area of personal weakness. I sensed that He wanted to do a work in my life in this area, and He gave me a passage that fit it perfectly.

I set aside a page in my prayer journal for each family member. I print out the prayer theme (or verse) the Lord has shown me for each one, along with a specific prayer outline that focuses on the major issues, such as spiritual life, work, school, relationships, and health. I leave plenty of blank lines to add special needs and to record God's answers.

I put a snapshot of each family member at the top of his or her page. It is a great blessing to look at these faces during my morning quiet time as I pray according to God's agenda for them.

My prayers for my family have become more focused, more scriptural, and more effective as a result of discovering God's prayer agenda for them. And while I'm still learning to intercede for my loved ones, here are some things I've found helpful so far.

Begin with a prayer retreat early in the year.

To discover God's prayer agenda, I need to get away, just the Lord and me. Though I try to take several prayer retreats every year, the one at the beginning of the year seems most important for this purpose.

On the retreat, spend concentrated time praying for each loved one.

As I pray for my family, the Lord sensitizes me to their needs and the particular challenges for them in the year ahead. I keep my journal (or my laptop computer) close at hand so I can take notes on any impressions He brings to mind.

Ask God for a theme for each loved one.

Don't forget to wait for His answer! When I submit myself to God's Word, confess known sin, and ask for His protection and control in my life, I can wait confidently for Him to answer. I don't hear an audible voice, but the Lord does impress my mind with specific guidance for each member of my family. Sometimes I'm surprised by the passage of Scripture He leads me to. Other times He directs me to promises I'm already claiming for them.

Develop a prayer outline for each loved one.

Having prayed at length for family members, my heart and mind seem better prepared to develop individual prayer outlines for them. I include daily concerns, like work and school, along with eternal ones, like time in the Word and Christian character formation. The Lord helps bring the right emphasis for each one. I've discovered that praying for my family is a dynamic process. The outline serves as a guide for my intercession, one that the Lord often adjusts, changes, or expands, as I pray daily for each person.

Summarize the "prayer agenda" for each family member in your journal.

After I get back from my retreat, I put everything

197

together on a single page, front and back, for each loved one. The picture goes at the top, then the passage or promise God gave me. Then comes the outline for what I'll pray each day. Finally, I add blank lines to record additional requests and God's answers through the year.

Let family members know how and when you're praying for them.

I usually write a letter to my sons while I'm still on my prayer retreat. I resist the temptation to make it sound like I've just returned from the mountain with stone tablets in hand! But I do want them to know that I've been meeting with God on their behalf, and about how I'll be praying for them in the year ahead.

These days there is a lot of teaching on the importance of a "prayer shield" for Christian leaders. It's true—pastors, missionaries, and other leaders need teams of intercessors to pray for them. But interceding for our families is also a high calling. Discovering the Lord's prayer agenda for my family has helped me pray for their deepest needs and ask for His highest purposes for their lives. I hope it will do the same in your family.

JIM CARPENTER is the vice president of communications for Dynamic Church Planting International. This article is taken from *Pray!*, Issue 29, pp. 26-28.